ECONOMIC
CHOICES
1984

ALICE M. RIVLIN *Editor*

ECONOMIC CHOICES 1984

Henry J. Aaron
Barry P. Bosworth
Linda Cohen
Harvey Galper
William W. Kaufmann
Lawrence B. Krause
Robert Z. Lawrence
Robert H. Meyer
Alice M. Rivlin
Louise B. Russell

THE BROOKINGS INSTITUTION
Washington, D.C.

Copyright © 1984 by
THE BROOKINGS INSTITUTION
1775 Massachusetts Avenue, N.W., Washington, D.C. 20036

ISBN 0-8157-7488-5 (cloth)
ISBN 0-8157-7487-7 (paper)

Library of Congress Catalog Card Number 84-71381

9 8 7 6 5 4 3 2 1

THE BROOKINGS INSTITUTION is an independent organization devoted to nonpartisan research, education, and publication in economics, government, foreign policy, and the social sciences generally. Its principal purposes are to aid in the development of sound public policies and to promote public understanding of issues of national importance.

The Institution was founded on December 8, 1927, to merge the activities of the Institute for Government Research, founded in 1916, the Institute of Economics, founded in 1922, and the Robert Brookings Graduate School of Economics and Government, founded in 1924.

The Board of Trustees is responsible for the general administration of the Institution, while the immediate direction of the policies, program, and staff is vested in the President, assisted by an advisory committee of the officers and staff. The by-laws of the Institution state: "It is the function of the Trustees to make possible the conduct of scientific research, and publication, under the most favorable conditions, and to safeguard the independence of the research staff in the pursuit of their studies and in the publication of the results of such studies. It is not a part of their function to determine, control, or influence the conduct of particular investigations or the conclusions reached."

The President bears final responsibility for the decision to publish a manuscript as a Brookings book. In reaching his judgment on the competence, accuracy, and objectivity of each study, the President is advised by the director of the appropriate research program and weighs the views of a panel of expert outside readers who report to him in confidence on the quality of the work. Publication of a work signifies that it is deemed a competent treatment worthy of public consideration but does not imply endorsement of conclusions or recommendations.

The Institution maintains its position of neutrality on issues of public policy in order to safeguard the intellectual freedom of the staff. Hence interpretations or conclusions in Brookings publication should be understood to be solely those of the authors and should not be attributed to the Institution, to its trustees, officers, or other staff members, or to the organizations that support its research.

Foreword

By ADOPTING economic policies that resulted in large federal deficits and high interest rates, the United States has made a poor choice. Sharp reductions in these deficits would improve the chances for economic growth and restore the ability of U.S. industries to compete in world markets. But deficits cannot be brought down without cutting spending and raising taxes. The choices are painful.

The authors of this volume present a plan that would not only reduce deficits but also increase future flexibility in domestic spending, improve the effectiveness of defense expenditures, and reform the federal tax system. They also offer suggestions for coping with structural change in American industry and reversing recent increases in poverty. They offer their plan as a contribution to the national debate on economic choices that is sure to occur during the 1984 election campaign and in the next Congress.

The contributors to this volume are all members of the staff of the Economic Studies program at Brookings except for William W. Kaufmann, who is a consultant to the Foreign Policy Studies program and a member of the faculty of the Massachusetts Institute of Technology.

The authors are grateful to the following for helpful comments and criticisms on earlier drafts of these chapters: Alan J. Auerbach, Marc Bendick, Jr., Martin Binkin, Gary Burtless, Sheldon V. Danziger, Larry L. Dildine, Peter Edelman, Robert J. Flanagan, Irwin V. Garfinkel, Paul B. Ginsburg, Peter Gottschalk, Daphne T. Greenwood, Daniel I. Halperin, Robert W.

Hartman, Charles R. Hulten, Malcolm C. Lovell, Jr., Robert Lucke, Richard A. Musgrave, Joseph A. Pechman, Paul R. Portney, Robert D. Reischauer, Fred H. Sanderson, William Spring, Emil M. Sunley, Eric J. Toder, and Paul Van de Water.

Research assistance was provided by Shannon P. Butler, Paula R. DeMasi, Joseph P. Ferrie, Julia A. Henel, Julia L. Leighton, Gail C. Morton, and Patricia J. Regan. Secretarial assistance was provided by Gloria A. Adams, Charlotte Kaiser, Valerie M. Owens, Jacquelyn G. Sanks, Fredricka H. Stewart, Evelyn M. E. Taylor, Susan L. Woollen, and Kathleen Elliott Yinug. The risk of factual error was minimized by the work of Carolyn A. Rutsch and Alan G. Hoden. The manuscript was edited by Nancy D. Davidson, James R. Schneider, and Caroline Lalire.

This study was financed in part by grants from the John D. and Catherine T. MacArthur Foundation and from the Ford Foundation.

The views expressed here are those of the authors and should not be ascribed to the foundations whose assistance is acknowledged above, or to the trustees, officers, or other staff members of the Brookings Institution or to the other organizations with which the authors are affiliated.

BRUCE K. MACLAURY
President

May 1984
Washington, D.C.

Contents

Tables

Figure

1

Overview

HIGH DEFICITS in the federal budget, together with high interest rates, are endangering the future growth of the U.S. economy and undermining the ability of American industry to compete in world markets. Change is needed. The federal deficit should be drastically reduced—indeed eliminated by the end of the decade—and interest rates should be lowered. Reducing the deficit will increase the resources available for investment and improve the chances for healthy economic growth. It will also allow interest rates to come down, reduce the value of the dollar in foreign exchange markets, and make American products more competitive.

Cutting the federal deficit will be painful. Spending growth must be reduced and taxes raised. But the need to reduce the deficit also creates an opportunity to reassess the priorities of the federal government. We believe that the domestic spending programs of the federal government can be made more effective, defense objectives can be attained at substantially lower cost, and a thorough overhaul of the federal tax system can make it both fairer and more favorable to economic growth than the present system.

The United States also needs new policies to facilitate economic change. In a growing economy, people and resources must move from less productive to more productive pursuits. Public policy should make these changes less painful, not retard them. It should foster innovation and help dislocated workers find new jobs. It should help the poor and the less skilled move into the mainstream of American society.

This volume focuses on some of the economic choices facing

the nation in 1984 and lays out a package of proposals designed to enhance growth and facilitate change. It discusses why deficits should be cut and interest rates lowered. It proposes a plan for reducing the growth of domestic and defense spending and suggests a new system of federal taxation. It deals with changes in trade and labor market policy that could help adjustment to economic change and offers ways of assisting low-income people.

Why Growth Matters

Sustained economic growth should be a high priority of public policy. We should aim for an economy in which average incomes rise gradually over the years so that more is available for the satisfaction of both public and private needs. In the short run, as the economy recovers from the recession, rising incomes can be achieved by reducing unemployment and increasing the utilization of factories and other resources that were not used to capacity in the recession. Over the longer run, rising incomes require increases in productivity—output per worker has to rise.

In a growing economy public choices are less agonizing and divisive. It is possible to modernize the armed forces; keep the nation's infrastructure in repair; provide for the elderly, the sick, and the needy; improve education and other public services; and still have private incomes that rise after taxes. Public choices are never easy, but they generate far more conflict in a declining or stagnating economy, when an increase in the resources to meet one kind of need requires an absolute reduction of resources used to meet other needs.

Modern economies must undergo a continuous process of adaptation to new technologies and changing preferences of consumers. That change can involve serious hardship for workers and communities that have become dependent upon older, declining industries. But if overall employment is high and the economy is growing, it is much easier for workers in declining industries to find new jobs and for new firms to spring up to replace those that are in decline. It is less difficult for young people to acquire experience and get established in careers.

Moreover, the experience of the postwar period indicates that overall economic growth is a powerful means of reducing poverty. Programs to provide education and job skills for low-income people have little chance of success if there are few jobs available and little prospect of a better income. Even if some proportion of those in poverty cannot be expected to participate in income growth, the provision of resources for their support is easier with a growing economy.

No economy can grow every year or at a steady rate. Moreover, rapid growth increases the risk of inflation. The goal of policy should be to get the economy on a moderate growth path, aiming for real growth in the neighborhood of 4 percent a year on the average, and moderating the fluctuations around the trend.

Factors Favorable to Growth

The rate of growth in real output is currently strong as the economy emerges from the deep recession of the early 1980s. Yet there are grave doubts that the expansion can be sustained in future years and fears that the economy could return to the weak growth and poor productivity performance that characterized the 1970s.

Actually, however, there were several factors that contributed to poor economic performance in the 1970s that seem unlikely to recur in the near future. One such strain on the economy was the rapid increase in the labor force, which grew by about 45 percent between 1965 and 1980. Most of the newcomers were inexperienced young people—the baby boom generation growing up—and others were married women with relatively little job experience entering the work force in increasing numbers. The economy absorbed this influx, but at some cost to productivity growth.

Two rounds of energy price increases in the 1970s raised costs and necessitated considerable industrial retooling to save energy. The energy price rises precipitated rapid inflation as business passed on costs to consumers and workers sought higher wages to compensate for rising prices. Inflationary expectations caused consumers and businesses to act in ways that further aggravated inflationary pressures, and inflation proved extremely hard to control.

At the same time the economy was absorbing an explosion of regulation designed to protect the health and safety of workers and consumers, reduce environmental pollution, conserve energy, and promote equality of opportunity. This regulation helped make America a better place to live, but at the cost of some slowing of industrial growth and some aggravation of inflation.

These four factors—a labor force increase, energy price shocks, increased regulation, and stubborn inflation—are by no means the whole explanation for the slow increases in output and decline in productivity growth that affected not only the United States but most of the major industrial countries of the world in the 1970s. But they contributed to these developments, and fortunately they seem unlikely to recur in the near future. For the next few years, the United States will have an increasingly experienced labor force with relatively small numbers of untrained new entrants. Energy prices seem unlikely to rise rapidly unless there is a major conflict in the Middle East. Moreover, the United States now uses energy more efficiently than it did a decade ago and is far less dependent on imported oil. No major increases in regulation are in sight; indeed, regulation is being reduced in some areas. Inflation has been brought down from the double-digit levels of the late 1970s to rates of 4 to 5 percent a year. The reduction in inflation was purchased at great cost in unemployment and lost income in the 1980–82 recession, but it did occur. Barring outside shocks or excessive demand pressures, inflation seems likely to remain in the moderate range for at least the next few years.

If these four factors told the whole story, the outlook for growth in the next few years would be more favorable than it was in the 1970s. Unfortunately, the favorable outlook is threatened by an unfavorable policy: high federal deficits that reduce national saving, put upward pressure on interest rates, and prevent the accumulation of private capital necessary to sustain the expansion of output in future years.

The Outlook: High Deficits and High Interest Rates

For the last several years, monetary and fiscal policies—the two principal instruments by which the federal government affects the overall state of the economy—have worked at cross-purposes. Monetary policy has been predominantly restrictive; fiscal policy, predominantly stimulative. The result has been high interest rates and high deficits that will continue in the foreseeable future if policies are not changed.

Beginning in 1979, the monetary authorities, deeply concerned about the high inflation of the late 1970s, assiduously restricted the growth in the money supply. Interest rates rose to extremely high levels, and the economy went into a deep and lengthy recession from which it did not begin to recover until the end of 1982. Not surprisingly, the interest-rate-sensitive sectors of the economy were especially hard hit. Unemployment rose to over 10 percent of the labor force, while inflation dropped dramatically.

Meanwhile, fiscal policy was dominated by major reductions in personal and corporate income taxes that were enacted in 1981 and took effect during 1981–83. The revenue cuts were not matched by spending cuts, although the mix of spending shifted away from domestic programs and toward spending for defense and interest on the rising debt. As a result of both the recession and the cut in taxes without a corresponding cut in spending, the federal deficit soared to $193 billion, or 6 percent of GNP, in fiscal year 1983.

Since the end of 1982 the economy has been experiencing a healthy recovery that has affected all major sectors except net exports. Forecasters anticipate a 5 percent real increase in GNP in 1984 with declining unemployment and inflation remaining at a moderate rate of 4 to 5 percent.

Even if the economy continues to grow, however, the deficit in the federal budget will not decline unless current policies are changed. Although revenues will rise as the economy expands, spending will rise even faster, and the deficit will continue to increase. Even if the economy grew steadily through 1989 (as assumed in the projections of the Congressional Budget Office), unemployment fell to 6.5 percent, and interest rates declined, the deficit would still climb from about $200 billion in fiscal year 1985 (5.0 percent of GNP) to about $300 billion in 1989 (5.7 percent of GNP). This prospect of a rising deficit in an improving economy makes the situation very different from any experienced in the past. Since World War II high deficits have been associated with recession.

These projected deficits are not attributable to the social security and medicare trust funds, which, taken together, are expected to be roughly in balance through 1989, thanks to recent increases in payroll taxes. The problem is in the rest of the budget. Spending for programs other than medicare and social security will total about 17.2 percent of GNP in 1985 and will rise slightly faster than GNP, with defense and interest dominating the increase. However, the corresponding revenues, which were sharply reduced by the income tax cuts passed in 1981, will be only about 12.7 percent of GNP in 1985 and will rise slightly slower than GNP. Hence the large and widening gap.

Government borrowing to finance the deficit is contributing to the high level of interest rates and can be expected to exert more upward pressure in the future as private credit demands increase. As workers and factories become more fully employed, the monetary authorities will have to keep a tight rein on credit to avoid a reescalation of inflation. The conflict between a stimulative budget policy and a restrictive monetary policy will intensify, and interest rates are likely to rise further.

Why Policy Must Be Changed

Budget deficits in the anticipated range will absorb about two-thirds of the net private savings expected to be available, leaving less for capital formation. To put the matter slightly differently, federal government dissaving will offset a large part of the saving of other sectors of the economy. While it is possible that saving by other sectors could rise to offset the dissaving of the federal government, private saving has been a remarkably constant fraction of GNP over several decades. It is more likely that federal dissaving of such unprecedented magnitudes will diminish the domestic resources available for investment in plant, equipment, and housing and will drive up interest rates.

High deficits and high interest rates do not necessarily mean immediate disaster for the economy. The deficits will continue to stimulate the economy generally, while the high interest rates will tend to slow particular types of spending, especially housing and business investment. The result will be a shift in the mix of total spending—more resources for consumption, less for investment and housing. A low level of investment in plant and equipment is likely to reduce productivity increases and hamper economic growth in the longer run. Penalizing investment is borrowing from the future to increase consumption now.

Moreover, high interest rates have already had devastating effects on the ability of U.S. industry to compete in world markets. High rates have attracted a large inflow of capital from abroad. This foreign capital has helped finance the federal deficit as well as private investment, but has added to the demand for dollars on foreign exchange markets. The exchange value of the dollar has risen sharply in the last several years, which has made U.S. exports expensive for foreigners and foreign goods and services cheap for Americans. As a result, the United States has been running a huge deficit in its balance of trade; output and employment in industries facing foreign competition have suffered. Borrowing from abroad is also borrowing from the future for current consumption, since these debts to foreigners will have to be repaid with interest out of future national production.

High interest rates in the United States lead to high interest rates around the world and greatly aggravate the precarious international debt situation. As interest rates rise, third world countries find it increasingly difficult to meet the interest payments on their debts to U.S. banks.

In sum, we believe that the current mix of fiscal and monetary policy is a mistake. High deficits and high interest rates retard economic growth, damage U.S. competitiveness in world markets, and add to the strain on international credit. The United States should take action to lower the federal deficit and to bring interest rates down.

It is important that action be taken soon. At high interest rates the rising debt adds rapidly to the interest cost of the federal government. A $200 billion deficit at 10 percent interest adds $20 billion a year in increased interest costs. The longer the delay in cutting the deficit, the more taxes will have to be raised or spending cut.

The Necessity for Political Compromise

The economy would greatly benefit from a major switch in monetary and fiscal policies in which low deficits and low interest rates would replace high deficits and high interest rates. Making the switch, however, will be a severe test of U.S. governmental institutions. The painful actions necessary to cut the deficits will arouse strong political opposition. While concern about the deficits is widely expressed, specific proposals to raise taxes or cut domestic or defense programs are likely to encounter far more opposition than support. It will take political courage, ingenuity, and vision to fashion a deficit-reduction plan that will be widely regarded as fair and worthy of support even though specific elements are painful.

Moreover, making the policy switch will not only require compromise between the president and the Congress, but it will also necessitate an unusual degree of coordination between monetary and fiscal decisionmakers. If the switch is to be made without slowing the economy unduly as the deficit falls, the monetary authorities will have to allow a substantial reduction in interest rates and the exchange value of the dollar.

While we believe a strong economic case can be made for reducing the deficit, the choices among ways to do it depend on value judgments about federal spending priorities and the desirable size and role of government. Moreover, the required changes are so large that to approach a balance in the budget solely by increasing taxes would require unprecedented tax rate increases, while to accomplish the goal solely by cutting defense spending would threaten national security and to attain it solely by reducing domestic spending would gut basic government programs on which millions of people depend.

Hence for practical reasons a politically acceptable program to reduce the deficit must contain three elements: cuts in both domestic and defense spending and increases in revenues. The compromise should be seen as fair and evenhanded, requiring sacrifices from a broad range of taxpayers and beneficiaries of government programs, but not bearing too heavily on any one group.

We also believe that the necessity to cut the deficit should be an opportunity to reassess priorities and to make government programs more effective. The requirement to raise more revenue creates a timely moment for reforming the federal tax system, since raising substantial additional income tax revenue without reform would exacerbate the inequities and inefficiencies of the present system. Nevertheless, reform and reassessment take time, while action to reduce the deficit should be taken soon. Therefore, a two-stage plan seems in order: a set of simple evenhanded measures should be taken quickly, followed by more thorough efforts at reform. The plan described below has both these elements.

A Compromise Plan

The plan offered here is an attempt by a group of economists to lay out a feasible, fair blueprint for bringing the federal budget close to balance by 1989. It involves reduction in the growth of both domestic and defense spending and increases in revenue. The proposals for domestic spending and tax reform are in two stages. A short-run freeze on domestic spending to save money quickly would be followed by more basic restructuring of domestic programs. Similarly, tax changes designed to raise more revenue quickly by broadening the tax base and imposing a surtax would be followed by a thorough reform of the current federal tax system. The defense spending proposals, while not formally in two stages, also call for immediate cuts in weapons systems deemed duplicative or related to questionable objectives and a longer-run shift to a more moderate and sustainable pace of defense investment. The outlines of the plan, discussed in more detail below and in subsequent chapters, may be seen in table 1-1.

Our objective was to design a plan that would bring the

Table 1-1. *Proposed Deficit Reduction Plan, Fiscal Years 1985–89*
Billions of dollars

Item	1985	1986	1987	1988	1989
Baseline deficit[a]	−197	−217	−245	−272	−308
Proposed legislative actions[b]	40	80	120	160	200
Cuts in spending growth	17	41	59	77	92
Nondefense[c]	15	30	36	41	46
Short-run (freeze)	15	21	22	23	23
Long-run	. . .	9	14	18	23
Defense[d]	2	11	23	36	46
Tax increase[e]	23	39	61	83	108
Interest saving[b]	12	28	43	66	88
Resulting deficit	−145	−109	−82	−46	−20

a. Congressional Budget Office, *Baseline Budget Projections for Fiscal Years 1985–1989* (Government Printing Office, February 1984), and subsequent revisions.
b. See chap. 2.
c. See chap. 3.
d. These figures represent the difference between the CBO baseline defense outlays and the sum of the "efficient Reagan" defense outlays discussed in chap. 4 plus nonmilitary defense-related expenditures not included in the chap. 4 calculations.
e. See chap. 5.

federal budget into approximate balance by 1989. According to CBO estimates, current policies will produce a deficit in that year of over $300 billion, even under the relatively optimistic CBO economic assumptions. Hence the task was to agree on a set of legislative proposals to cut spending or raise revenues that, together with the likely reduction in federal interest costs that would accompany such cuts in the deficit, would save about $300 billion in 1989.

We started by designing a set of cuts in domestic spending growth that seemed feasible and likely to be regarded as fair in the context of an overall deficit-reduction plan. The short-run and long-run savings proposed were estimated to save $46 billion in 1989. We also examined the defense budget and identified an "efficient Reagan budget" that would achieve the defense objectives of the current administration at a lower cost. Coincidentally, this also would cut $46 billion from the CBO baseline in 1989.[1] We then estimated the tax increase that

1. Our defense calculations used the administration's price assumptions, while our estimates of savings in the other parts of the budget are based on CBO price assumptions. The result is likely to be an overestimate of the savings compared with the CBO baseline.

would be necessary, together with the interest saving, to get the deficit close to zero, and we set the tax rates in our proposed new federal tax system accordingly. When all the elements were put together, the estimated 1989 deficit turned out to be $20 billion.

We offer this set of proposals as an example of a feasible, fair plan to balance the budget in five years. The individual pieces of the plan would not necessarily be endorsed by each of us. Some of the elements can be defended on their merits, while others make sense only as part of a compromise plan to cut the deficit. All the elements would face strong political opposition from some quarter. But we believe that cutting the deficit is so important that normal political differences must be submerged in a common effort to achieve a goal that will benefit the whole economy.

Domestic Spending

Spending on domestic programs rose from less than 8 percent of GNP in fiscal 1962 to about 15 percent in 1980 as the federal government took on new responsibilities and raised spending for existing programs. Since 1980 this growth has slowed because of substantial cuts made in many programs. As these cuts continue to take effect and the economy recovers, domestic spending is expected to fall to about 13 percent of GNP by the end of the decade. In spite of the cuts already made, domestic spending must be reviewed again if the budget is to be brought into balance by 1989.

The choices about how to further restrain the growth in domestic spending will depend heavily on noneconomic value judgments about the appropriate size and mix of government activities, and these choices will require time for debate. We therefore propose a two-stage program to restrain domestic spending. The first stage is a one-year freeze in 1985, during which cost-of-living increases in benefits paid to individuals would be omitted unless prices rose more than 5 percent and appropriations for most other programs would be held at 1984 levels. Programs for low-income people would be exempted from the freeze. This modified freeze is a relatively simple and evenhanded way to reduce spending quickly, while allowing time for debate over the longer-term restructuring of domestic programs. It would save approximately $15 billion in 1985 and more than $20 billion each year during 1986–89.

The second stage would require more fundamental changes in domestic spending programs. We suggest a number of criteria to guide these changes.

—Steps should be taken to reduce somewhat the automatic growth in social security spending in order to give the political system more flexibility in the choice between social security benefit increases and other federal activities. These reductions should be achieved through changes in initial benefits, not in the cost-of-living adjustment.

—The new system of prospective rates for paying hospitals under medicare should be used to restrain the growth in costs to inflation plus 1 percent. Although this policy should be adequate for the next few years, further changes may be required in benefits or revenues if projections continue to indicate large deficits in the medicare trust fund by the mid-1990s.

—Both the civil service and military retirement systems should be changed to bring them more in line with private-sector pensions. For future retirees, initial benefits should be reduced somewhat below the levels that would be produced by the current systems, and full benefits should be available only at older ages than currently (sixty-two, for example). Benefits for current and future retirees should be only partially indexed for inflation.[2]

—Agricultural programs should be restructured to focus on stabilizing prices around long-term market-clearing levels. Deficiency payments should be ended and any new income supplements targeted to those in need.

—Spending on other domestic programs could be reduced

2. New civil service employees were covered by social security for the first time beginning in 1984. For others, the portion of their retirement benefit that corresponds to the social security benefits of private-sector workers should continue to be fully indexed for inflation.

through user charges, lower subsidies for some activities, or the elimination of some programs.

Paying for National Security

Because defense outlays account for about 30 percent of all federal spending and are rising faster than other spending, they are an obvious source of possible deficit reductions. Reducing the deficit at the expense of endangering national security, however, would be irresponsible. If we were convinced that the rapid defense buildup advocated by the Reagan administration were necessary to deter attack or deal effectively with threats to U.S. security, we would urge that it be continued and that its impact on the deficit be offset by higher taxes or cuts in other spending. We believe, however, that while the nation needs and can afford a strong defense, the Reagan defense program is not the best way of meeting that need. The rapid pace of the administration's defense buildup, especially the remarkable increase in procurement, is both unjustified and unwise. A more moderate and balanced growth could meet the administration's defense objectives more efficiently. Indeed, forces appropriate to an even higher level of perceived threat and a need for more immediate readiness could be purchased for less money than the administration is proposing to spend.

Simple percentage reductions in appropriations will not ensure that the remaining dollars are spent wisely and may in fact merely exacerbate some of the problems created by the Reagan defense plan by preventing neglected categories of expenditure from receiving their due. We offer instead a more prudent investment strategy that eliminates much of the duplication in the Reagan budget, eliminates expenditures designed to fulfill questionable objectives, and slows the overly rapid pace of investment, while achieving the same level of security at a significant saving in both outlays and future flexibility. In fact, such changes could save as much as $45 billion over what the administration is projecting in 1985 budget authority. We also present estimates of the cost of equally efficient budgets that address both higher and lower perceptions of the threat faced by the United States.

Reforming the Tax System

Increasing revenues by more than $100 billion in 1989 requires thorough reform of the current tax system. The corporation and individual income taxes are riddled with provisions that treat taxpayers inequitably and needlessly reduce economic efficiency. Raising revenue simply by raising tax rates would aggravate these problems.

Various approaches to reform are possible. Some would broaden the base of the individual income tax by ending most exclusions and deductions in order to obtain additional revenue without increasing tax rates. Others propose shifting part of the revenue structure from the taxation of income to taxation of consumption by enacting a value-added tax or national sales tax. Our proposal combines both ideas: broadening the base and taxing spending rather than income. We would replace both the individual income tax and the estate and gift tax with an individual cash flow tax on income from all sources minus net saving. With this base, reduced rates of 5 to 32 percent would impose burdens on each economic class similar to those generated by the current income and estate taxes. Somewhat higher rates would be required to raise the additional revenue called for in table 1-1. The corporation income tax would be replaced by a cash flow tax on corporate receipts minus current expenses, including investment. This new tax system would not be free of problems—no perfect tax exists—and some difficult transition issues must be resolved, but we believe it would be fairer, simpler, and more favorable to growth than the present system, while not shifting tax burdens among economic classes.

Such a major change in tax laws could not be put in place quickly enough to produce the added revenue needed to bring down the deficit in the next two or three years. We therefore propose an interim tax program combining some immediate broadening of the tax base with a temporary income tax surcharge.

Our approach to tax reform is, of course, not the only possible approach. Almost any comprehensive income tax reform would permit considerable progress to be made toward improving fairness, promoting economic efficiency, and facilitating administration.

We believe, however, that a cash flow tax on individuals and corporations would go farther than the commonly proposed alternatives, such as a flat-rate tax or a value-added tax, toward achieving simultaneously all the goals of a desirable tax system. It would impose tax burdens based on each person's lifetime command over resources. It would terminate the current capricious variations in business tax rates that distort investment decisions. It would reduce the scope for tax avoidance through tax shelters. It would ease compliance for those who face the greatest difficulty in determining their tax liabilities under current law. Finally, it is based on a consistent, logical framework for assessing tax burdens.

Adjusting to Economic Change

The major declines in employment in manufacturing and in net exports that the United States experienced in the 1980s were caused by recession and the high value of the dollar on foreign exchange markets. The evidence from the 1970s does not indicate that the United States has been deindustrializing, that the pace of structural change is accelerating, or that the United States is suffering from some fundamental disadvantage in international trade. Hence sustained growth and a lower value of the dollar can be expected to reduce the trade and structural unemployment problems of the country to manageable proportions.

But even in a growing economy the shifting of people and resources from less productive to more productive sectors will pose painful problems for some workers, firms, and communities. The government will be pressured to retard these painful changes through protectionism and other measures. But it would be short-sighted of the United States to try to prevent these changes from occurring by protecting or subsidizing inefficient industries. Instead, policies should be designed to facilitate change and to reduce the adverse effects on dislocated workers.

The administration has on occasion succumbed to pressures from inefficient sectors and has provided protection in the least efficient manner—quotas. Existing quotas and quotalike devices such as voluntary export restraints should be converted into tariffs. Where temporary protection is required by law, tariffs should be designed so that their levels decline automatically. At the same time the United States must also act vigorously to ensure that foreign markets are open to U.S. exporters.

If the United States is to improve its policies for adapting to structural change in markets, the costs and benefits of those policies must also be made clearer. Currently a welter of programs provides assistance to industries and labor in a haphazard and confusing fashion. A new government agency should be established to analyze and clarify the effects of these policies and to improve their coordination.

Although workers suffering prolonged unemployment as a result of economic dislocation will be a tiny fraction of the labor force in a period of sustained growth, their problems can be severe and deserve special attention. The United States should institute policies to improve workers' adaptability to structural change by training them in basic and vocational skills before they are laid off; it should also institute policies to match unemployed workers with available jobs more efficiently. Because different workers face different obstacles to reemployment, we recommend job search, relocation, and retraining programs designed to provide progressively greater assistance to individuals as their term of unemployment lengthens. The U.S. Employment Service should be thoroughly overhauled and expanded, and emergency teams should be created to assist local labor markets that experience closings of large plants.

Investment in research and development is also crucial for adapting to change and enhancing economic growth. Because the private market tends to underinvest in research activities, government policies to promote investment in research and development are necessary. Direct subsidies can be important for encouraging efficient investment in basic and applied research. Government support of commercially oriented development projects, however, is more problematic because political incentives are likely to generate poor project choices and management and to undermine the overall research and development effort.

Helping the Poor

Although the average American standard of living is high, not all share in the affluence. In 1982, 34 million people—15 percent of the population—lived in households with incomes below the government's official poverty line. Blacks, Hispanics, and families headed by women are overrepresented among the poor.

The incidence of poverty declined rapidly in the 1960s under the combined impact of strong economic growth and rising transfer payments. In the 1970s, however, poverty hardly declined at all. Slower growth and high unemployment offset the favorable effects of continued increases in transfer payments. After 1979 the incidence of poverty increased substantially, as cuts in the real value of public assistance and other transfer payments exacerbated the effect of the recession on low-income people.

Over the last two decades, dramatic improvements have been made in the income level of older people, largely as a result of increases in social security and other transfers. Although the elderly are a larger fraction of the total population than a decade or two ago, they are a smaller fraction of the poor.

A major change in the living arrangements of Americans—the increased prevalence of families headed by women—is disproportionately reflected among the poor. Women who head families are less likely than men to be in the labor force, and they have lower earnings. Families headed by nonelderly women now make up 43 percent of poor families. This "feminization" of poverty is worrisome because economic growth is unlikely to substantially reduce poverty in this group.

Even if the economy grows and unemployment declines, recent increases in poverty will be reversed very slowly unless policy is changed. We believe new efforts are needed.

In the short run the most direct approach to easing the plight of the poor is to increase benefits going directly to poor people, especially those programs that have failed to keep up with the cost of living. We propose establishing a national minimum benefit for aid to families with dependent children, increasing food stamp benefits, extending medicaid benefits to all poor families with children, and increasing the earned-income tax credit. We also suggest shifting more of the cost of support of low-income children onto absent parents.

If overall unemployment continues to fall, the next few years may offer a unique opportunity to break the cycle of poverty by concentrating on improving the education, training, job experience, and motivation of low-income youth. In the late 1980s and early 1990s, there will be relatively few new entrants into the labor force. The chances that low-income youth who complete high school can obtain and hold jobs should improve. We suggest concentrating on helping this age group and assisting low-income parents to earn enough to move their families out of poverty.

2

Lowering the Deficits and Interest Rates

U.S. FISCAL and monetary policies are currently creating large budget deficits and high real interest rates. This combination of policies is bad for economic growth and U.S. ability to compete in world markets. Future growth is likely to be retarded because the continuing high deficits now in prospect will reduce the share of national output available for both business investment and housing below that which prevailed in the 1960s and 1970s. The deficits also contribute to the dollar's high value in world markets, which is already causing severe damage to U.S. exports and to import-competing industries. Moreover, high U.S. interest rates complicate the economic policies of other countries and make it difficult for third world nations to service their debts.

Future monetary and fiscal policy should be aimed at promoting sustained noninflationary rates of economic growth. This means switching from policies of high deficits and high interest rates to ones that will lower deficits and interest rates. The federal deficit, now projected at about 5 percent of GNP in 1987, should be reduced to about 2 percent by then and should approach balance by the end of the decade. Monetary policy should allow interest rates to fall so as to offset the reduction in demand that would accompany the reduction in the deficit.

This chapter discusses how the high deficits and high interest

Barry P. Bosworth undertook primary responsibility for drafting this chapter.

rates came about, why they threaten growth and competitiveness, and what can be done about them.

Monetary and Fiscal Policy at Cross-Purposes

In recent years monetary policy and fiscal policy have been directed toward different goals. Since 1979 monetary policy has been aimed primarily at reducing inflation by restraining the growth of money and credit. Fiscal policy did not contribute to this restraint, and since late 1982 it has been highly stimulative. The conflict between the two sets of policies has led to high real interest rates, which could rise further as the economy continues to recover from the recession and the flow of saving into the United States from abroad begins to slacken.

The escalating inflation of the late 1970s was disruptive to the economy and raised fears of a continuing inflationary spiral. After 1979 the monetary authorities, driven by a deep concern about inflation, pursued a policy of severe restraint—slowing inflation by reducing demand, production, and employment. The Federal Reserve established very restrictive targets for the growth of the money supply, measured both narrowly (M1) and broadly (M2). An unexpectedly sharp contraction of economic activity in the first half of 1980 led the Federal Reserve to back off somewhat; but it returned to a policy of restraint in early 1981 that persisted until the summer of 1982.

Meanwhile, fiscal policy remained largely unchanged. Although the federal budget deficit increased from 1.5 percent of GNP in early 1980 to 3.7 percent in the second quarter of 1982, that change was a passive response to the recession, which had reduced revenues and increased outlays for unemployment benefits and similar programs. Discretionary changes in the budget are more accurately reflected in a cyclically adjusted measure of the deficit, as shown in figure 2-1a. On that basis there was a small movement toward stimulus in the middle of 1981 as a result of the business tax reductions; but that stimulus was largely offset by concurrent reductions in nondefense expenditures. The major elements of the budget program adopted in 1981 were delayed to late 1982 and 1983, when the two large reductions in personal taxes took effect. The scheduled defense buildup had a limited initial effect on the economy because of long lags between the decision to authorize new programs and the actual increase in economic activity, while the cuts in civilian spending took effect quickly.[1] Thus the initial effect of the combined expenditure changes was to lower the deficit.

The effects of these conflicting economic policies were evident in financial markets. The competition between the government and the private sector for a severely restricted supply of credit pushed interest rates up very sharply (see figure 2-1b). Between mid-1978 and mid-1981 the short-term Treasury bill rate more than doubled from 8 percent to 17 percent, and the long-term bond rate rose from 8 percent to 15 percent. While short-term interest rates have now declined to about 10 percent, the long-term rate has remained at nearly 12 percent. The change is particularly dramatic when the short-term interest rate is adjusted for inflation (the real interest rate). The real interest rate increased from a negative 2 percent in 1978 to 8 to 9 percent in 1981, and it continues at a historically high level of 5 to 6 percent.[2]

Monetary restraint dominated the course of the economy throughout the 1979–82 period. The monetary authorities stuck by their anti-inflation program, interest rates rose sharply, and the economy slid into a long-drawn-out recession. As shown in figure 2-1c, the decline in demand was heavily concentrated in interest-sensitive sectors such as residential construction, business investment, consumer durables, and net exports.[3] In

1. The program was explained as expanding supply-side incentives, but the specific actions added up to the largest peacetime package of traditional demand-stimulus measures. While there was little net increased fiscal stimulus in the first year, the 1981 decisions set up a major conflict with monetary policy in 1985 and beyond.

2. The real short-term interest rate averaged −0.7 percent in the 1950s, 1.6 percent in the late 1960s, and −0.4 percent in the 1970s. It is more difficult to adjust long-term interest rates because of the lack of a measure of expected long-term price changes. However, long-term rates have been unusually high relative to the short-term rate in the current recovery.

3. These sectors always bear the brunt of any recession because they are postponable expenditures. But the magnitude of the decline was larger in the 1980–82 period. In the recession trough of the fourth quarter of 1982, the share of GNP devoted to fixed investment, consumer durables, and net exports was 10 percent below the average share at comparable points of previous postwar business cycles.

Figure 2-1. *Indicators of Economic Activity, 1976–83*

Percent of gross national product

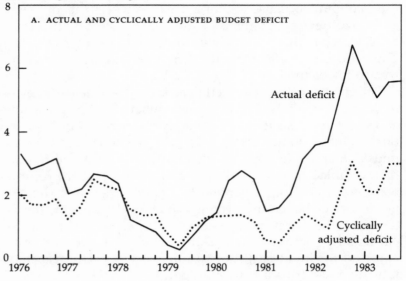

A. ACTUAL AND CYCLICALLY ADJUSTED BUDGET DEFICIT

Actual deficit

Cyclically
adjusted deficit

Percent

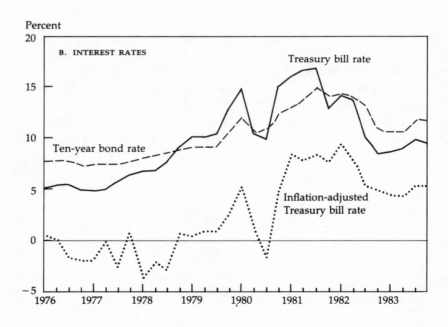

B. INTEREST RATES

Treasury bill rate

Ten-year bond rate

Inflation-adjusted
Treasury bill rate

Figure 2-1 (*continued*)

Index 1979:4 = 100

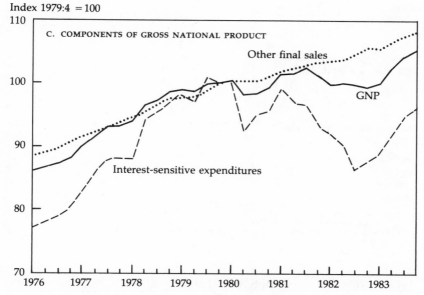

Sources: The cyclically adjusted budget deficit is based on a GNP consistent with a constant 6 percent unemployment rate and is obtained from U.S. Department of Commerce, Bureau of Economic Analysis, *Survey of Current Business* (December 1983), p. 26. Interest-sensitive expenditures include residential construction, business fixed investment, consumer durables, and net exports. Treasury bill rates are expressed as bond-equivalent yields and are calculated from data published in Board of Governors of the Federal Reserve System, *Federal Reserve Bulletin*, various issues.

the second half of 1982 expenditures on those items were 12 percent below their 1979 peak, while spending in other categories continued to expand. The growth in total GNP averaged less than 0.5 percent annually between the end of 1979 and 1982, while industrial production declined by 11 percent, unemployment rose from 5.8 percent to 10.7 percent, and the utilization of industrial capacity fell below 70 percent.

The deep recession of 1980–82 clearly slowed inflation, as the monetary authorities intended. In that respect the policy succeeded. As shown in table 2-1, consumer price inflation dropped from an average of 12.7 percent in 1979–80 to 3.3 percent in 1983. Several special factors, in addition to the recession, contributed to that decline. Most important was the sharp drop in energy prices: the average retail price of energy grew at a 25 percent annual rate during 1979–80, but fell by 0.5 percent in 1983. Furthermore, the 33 percent rise in the

Table 2-1. *Measures of Inflation and Unemployment, 1978–83*[a]
Percent

Measure	1978	1979	1980	1981	1982	1983
Actual inflation rate						
Consumer price index (CPI)	9.0	12.8	12.6	9.6	4.4	3.3
GNP fixed weight deflator	8.9	9.3	10.3	8.9	4.9	4.3
Underlying inflation rate						
CPI minus food, energy, and shelter	6.6	7.6	9.6	8.7	6.1	4.2
Average hourly earnings index	8.4	8.0	9.6	8.4	5.9	3.9
Employment cost index	7.7	8.7	9.0	8.8	6.3	5.0
Unemployment[b]						
Total	6.0	5.8	7.0	7.5	9.5	9.6
Whites	5.2	5.1	6.3	6.7	8.6	8.4
Minorities	11.9	11.3	13.1	14.2	17.3	17.8

Source: Author's calculations based on data from Bureau of Labor Statistics, Department of Labor, and Bureau of Economic Analysis, Department of Commerce.
a. Change measured between the fourth quarters of the prior year and the current year.
b. Average for the year.

dollar exchange rate between June 1980 and the end of 1983 sharply lowered the price of all imported goods, further cutting the inflation rate.[4] A more realistic measure of the fundamental improvement is provided by looking at domestic wage costs or price indexes that exclude imported goods and volatile commodity prices. On that basis domestic inflation has declined from an annual rate of about 10 percent to a range of 4 to 5 percent. But the costs of the anti-inflation program were very high. Unemployment increased from 6 to 10 percent, and the income of the average person was reduced substantially: the recession cost the United States over $600 billion in lost income during 1980–83.

Whether the benefits (lower inflation) were worth the costs (high unemployment) is a controversial issue. For the most part Congress and the administration verbally supported the monetary policy of the Federal Reserve. Yet the failure to adopt similar measures for fiscal policy exacerbated the pressures on interest rates and concentrated the burden on those sectors most affected by interest rates.

4. The exchange rate measure used here is a bilateral trade-weighted index compiled by Morgan Guaranty Trust.

The Outlook under Current Policies

Reduced concerns about domestic inflation and increased problems in international financial markets both contributed to an easing of monetary policy in mid-1982 and a greater willingness on the part of the Federal Reserve to finance an economic expansion. Money supply growth was allowed to accelerate from an annual average of 5.8 percent from the end of 1980 through the second quarter of 1982 to 11.8 percent over the next four quarters. Furthermore, although fiscal policy had not joined in the prior restraint, it became highly expansionary following large tax cuts in July 1982 and July 1983.

These shifts in fiscal and monetary policy have in combination initiated a strong economic recovery. Interest rates have declined substantially although real rates have declined little. Economic growth in 1983, led by a surge in consumer spending and home building, exceeded prior expectations. Fears that the decline in interest rates would be insufficient to encourage expenditures on housing, consumer durables, and business investment proved to be unfounded. In fact, the 6 percent rate of real GNP growth during 1983 was very much in line with the average experience during the first year of recovery from other postwar recessions. The unemployment rate—in part because of an unexpectedly slow growth of the labor force—declined by a record 2.5 percentage points in only twelve months, and inflation continued to slow.

The outlook is for continued growth. The government is anticipating an expansion of real GNP of about 5 percent during 1984. And, although unemployment will decline less rapidly in 1984 than in 1983, it should approach 7 percent by year-end. Meanwhile, inflation is projected at a modest 4 to 5 percent.

In view of this outlook, one might ask what all the concern is about. In the near term, the large budget deficit is a powerful force for economic recovery and the overall economy is doing well. However, these policies threaten serious problems for the United States and the world economy if they are continued. Unless fiscal stimulus is reduced, the monetary authorities will face an increasingly severe dilemma as the economy approaches full employment in future years. To accommodate the extraordinary borrowing demands of the federal government by allowing a rapid money supply growth would threaten a recurrence of high inflation; but to pursue a monetary policy consistent with price stability would threaten a resurgence of higher interest rates, causing dislocation in the domestic economy and endangering the economies of debtor nations abroad. Even within the current economic environment, the Federal Reserve has been able to constrain the speed of recovery within noninflationary limits only at the cost of abnormally high interest rates. The high interest rates have contributed to an unbalanced recovery in which some sectors, particularly those facing international competition, have not participated.

The Budget Outlook

The current projections of the federal budget by the Congressional Budget Office (CBO) show a rise in the deficit, under current spending policies and tax rates, from $197 billion in fiscal year 1985 to $308 billion by the end of the decade (see table 2-2).[5] As a share of GNP, the deficit would rise from an average of 1.9 percent in the 1970s to an average of 5.5 percent in 1987–89. The cumulative effect of these budget deficits is reflected in a nearly fourfold rise in the public debt from $716 billion (28 percent of GNP) in 1980 to $2,636 billion (49 percent of GNP) in 1989.

Much of the budget deficit in 1983 was a product of the recession and the associated revenue losses, but that will not be true in later years. The CBO budget projections assume a continuation of the economic recovery with unemployment reduced to 6.5 percent by the end of the decade. Thus the growth in the budget deficit reflects a structural imbalance

---

5. The current services budget is based upon a continuation of current tax laws and expenditure programs except for a 5 percent annual real growth in budget authorizations for defense.

Table 2-2. *Federal Government Budget, Selected Fiscal Years, 1960–89*

Item	Actual				Projected		
	1960	1970	1980	1983	1985	1987	1989
Billions of dollars							
Receipts	93	193	517	601	733	863	1,016
Expenditures	92	196	577	796	930	1,109	1,324
Surplus or deficit	1	-3	-60	-193	-197	-245	-308
Public debt	237	285	716	1,143	1,538	2,028	2,636
Percent of GNP							
Receipts	18.6	19.9	20.1	18.6	18.7	18.7	18.9
Expenditures	18.5	20.2	22.4	24.7	23.8	24.0	24.6
Surplus or deficit	0.1	-0.3	-2.3	-6.1	-5.0	-5.3	-5.7
Public debt	47.6	29.4	27.8	35.4	39.3	44.0	49.0

Source: Congressional Budget Office, *An Analysis of the President's Budgetary Proposals for Fiscal Year 1985* (Government Printing Office, February 1984), p. 2.

between taxes and expenditures that cannot be solved by economic recovery.[6]

A perspective on the budget is provided in table 2-3, which shows expenditures and taxes as shares of GNP for both past and future years. First, despite the public focus on the rapid growth of the social security program, it is not the source of the future deficit problem. Although Congress previously legislated increases in retirees' benefits that are today the source of substantial political controversy, it also provided for their financing by increasing employment taxes. The growth of social security outlays will slow substantially in the future; and, with

6. The administration's projection of a current services budget deficit of $193 billion in 1989 differs in several respects from that of the CBO. The administration is slightly more optimistic about revenue growth, and its assumption of an inflation rate that averages about 0.5 percentage point annually below the CBO's figure helps hold down expenditures. However, a large portion of the difference in the projected deficits can be traced to the administration's assumption that interest rates will fall from 9 percent in 1983 to 5 percent in 1989 in the presence of extremely high annual deficits and a high utilization of resources in the private sector. The CBO projects a decline to 8 percent, and even that may be optimistic. Current long-term interest rates, for example, imply that investors are expecting interest rates to rise in future years. The extreme nature of the administration's interest rate assumptions has led us to rely upon the CBO projections.

Table 2-3. *Budget Revenues and Outlays as a Percentage of Gross National Product, Selected Fiscal Years, 1960–89*

Budget component	Actual				Projected		
	1960	*1970*	*1980*	*1983*	*1985*	*1987*	*1989*
Social security							
Taxes[a]	2.1	3.5	4.4	4.6	4.9	4.9	5.3
Outlays	2.3	3.1	4.6	5.3	4.9	4.7	4.6
Surplus or deficit	−0.1	0.3	−0.2	−0.7	0.1	0.2	0.6
Medicare							
Taxes[a]	. . .	0.5	0.9	1.1	1.2	1.3	1.3
Outlays	. . .	0.6	1.2	1.6	1.8	1.9	2.1
Surplus or deficit	. . .	−0.1	−0.3	−0.5	−0.6	−0.6	−0.8
General fund							
Receipts	16.4	16.0	14.8	12.9	12.7	12.5	12.3
Expenditures	16.2	16.4	16.5	17.7	17.2	17.4	17.9
Defense	9.7	8.4	5.2	6.5	6.7	7.1	7.6
Net interest	1.4	1.5	2.0	2.8	3.2	3.6	4.0
Nondefense	5.2	6.5	9.3	8.5	7.2	6.7	6.3
Surplus or deficit	0.2	−0.5	−1.6	−4.8	−4.5	−4.9	−5.6

Source: Calculated from data in Congressional Budget Office, *Baseline Budget Projections for Fiscal Years 1985–1989* (GPO, February 1984), as revised by the CBO.
a. Includes personal income taxation of benefits, but not transfers or interest payments from the general fund.

the legislation passed in 1983, the fund is projected to generate a substantial surplus throughout the remainder of the century.[7] The medicare program, however, faces serious problems. Expenditures continue to rise much faster than GNP, and over the 1980s the deficit in this fund will offset the surplus in social security.[8]

The basic problem of the deficit lies with the general fund.

7. The surplus will provide a reserve against unexpected future contingencies. In addition, it can be justified as a desirable means of reducing the burden caused by a rapid growth of the retired population in the next century. But it can do so only if the saving it generates is allowed to flow through into capital formation, increasing the capital stock and national income in future years. Those benefits will be lost if the government is allowed to use the social security surplus to finance a medicare or general fund deficit.

8. Unlike social security, the medicare program was not designed to be fully self-supporting, and 50 percent of the costs for the supplementary medical insurance were to be provided by general revenues. But premium increases were constrained after 1972, and by 1983 they covered only about 25 percent of program costs. In addition, the basic trust fund is projected to encounter serious financing problems in future years.

After remaining almost constant as a share of GNP between 1960 and 1980, expenditures are now projected to rise by 1.4 percentage points of overall GNP during the 1980s (from 16.5 to 17.9 percent). Meanwhile, taxes are being cut by over 2 percent of GNP as a result of the 1981 and 1982 tax acts. Thus the deficit in the general fund grows from 1.6 percent of GNP in 1980 to an average of 5 percent during 1986–89. By the end of the decade tax revenues will finance only two-thirds of general fund expenditures.

The redirection of budget priorities by the Reagan administration is also clearly evident in table 2-3. After declining from 9.7 to 5.2 percent of GNP over the two prior decades, defense expenditures are projected to rise to 7.6 percent of GNP by 1989. This buildup in defense is offset by an equivalent reduction in nondefense programs. After rising from 5.2 to 9.3 percent of GNP between 1960 and 1980, nondefense spending falls back to a 6.3 percent share by the end of the decade— below the levels of 1965. Net interest payments on the public debt, however, rise by a full 2 percent of GNP between 1980 and 1989 because of both the large budget deficits and high interest rates.

One of the most striking developments shown in table 2-3 is the steady decline over the last twenty years in the ratio of general fund taxes to GNP and the rise in the corresponding ratio for employment taxes (social security and medicare). Until 1981 that decline was the result of a slight increase in income tax rates that was offset by sharp cuts in effective corporate income and excise tax rates. Since then, income tax rates have also been reduced. In other words, the only major tax increase in the United States has been the payroll tax on labor income.[9]

The CBO's budget estimates are based on a highly optimistic set of economic projections. They assume that the United States

9. According to some studies, marginal tax rates on some types of capital income have increased in the United States; but, because of an increased tendency to exclude capital income from the tax base, effective marginal rates of taxation on capital have declined. See, for example, Eugene Steuerle, "Is Income from Capital Subject to Individual Income Taxation?" *Public Finance Quarterly*, vol. 10 (July 1982), pp. 283–303; and Don Fullerton and Yolanda K. Henderson, "Incentive Effects of Taxes on Income from Capital: Alternative Policies in the 1980s," presented at the Urban Institute Conference on Reagan's Economic Policies and Long-Term Growth, September 1983.

will experience a seven-year period without a recession and with declining unemployment, a steady or even falling rate of inflation, and a slight decline in interest rates from current levels. If the United States should encounter another recession or an upward movement of interest rates, the deficit will be far larger than indicated here.[10]

From an economic perspective the huge budget deficits have three principal causes: (1) the actions taken by the president and Congress in 1981 to cut taxes without a matching reduction in total outlays, (2) the recession of 1980–82, and (3) sustained high interest rates. Spending was simply shifted from nondefense to defense programs. The depth and the duration of the recession added to the public debt and that, together with high interest rates, will have a compound effect on the growth of interest payments in future years.

The importance of the legislative actions is highlighted in table 2-4. The first line shows the budget deficit that would have resulted, based on current economic assumptions, with the budget policies in effect in January 1981. Even under that budget, the recession would have produced large deficits during 1982–85. But the economic recovery would have restored a small budget surplus by 1989. Since 1981 the administration and Congress have initiated a sharp shift in the allocation of budget outlays. Overall program outlays, however, are not significantly altered. By 1989 the $77 billion rise in annual defense spending will almost precisely offset the cuts in nondefense programs. Despite the lack of overall expenditure reductions, the 1981 tax act reduced annual revenues by an amount that will exceed $300 billion annually by 1989. Since then Congress has enacted several offsetting tax increases, but 1989 tax revenues will still be $239 billion less than under the 1980 tax laws. Meanwhile, the cumulative additions to the public debt will add $100 billion to annual interest payments in 1989. Under current budget policies the deficit would continue to widen forever into the future, with or without economic recovery.

10. Some commentators try to dismiss the projected deficits by pointing out that forecasts of the deficit have been subject to large errors over the last decade. What they fail to mention is that actual deficits have been far larger than projected because of the optimism alluded to above.

Table 2-4. *Effects of Policy Changes since 1981 on Budget Deficits, Fiscal Years 1982–89*
Billions of dollars

Policy change	1982	1983	1984	1985	1986	1987	1988	1989
Projected surplus or deficit under policies in effect Jan. 1, 1981	−109	−148	−110	−85	−63	−36	−8	29
Legislative changes								
Defense spending increases	−1	−17	−25	−36	−42	−54	−65	−77
Nondefense spending cuts	39	46	48	59	71	74	76	78
Tax actions								
1981	−40	−91	−135	−166	−210	−248	−282	−321
1982	*	18	38	41	49	58	56	52
1983	*	1	3	8	10	11	22	30
Effect of legislative actions on interest costs	*	−2	−9	−19	−32	−49	−72	−100
Total changes	−2	−47	−79	−112	−154	−209	−264	−337
Projected surplus or deficit under policies in effect Jan. 1, 1984	−111	−195	−189	−197	−217	−245	−272	−308

Source: CBO, *Baseline Budget Projections for Fiscal Years 1985–1989*, pp. 115–16. The deficits for policies in effect in 1981 and 1984 are adjusted for revisions in the CBO projections since publication of the baseline projections in February 1984.
* Less than $500 million.

Hardly anyone in the administration or Congress explicitly advocates growing structural deficits as desirable fiscal policy for a recovering economy. Efforts to reduce the deficits, however, have failed because of conflicting views about spending priorities and the appropriate size of government. The administration supports measures to reduce the deficit by making further cuts in domestic spending. Many members of Congress believe that domestic spending has been cut enough and that efforts to reduce the deficit should concentrate on slowing the defense buildup and restoring revenues reduced by the tax cuts. Advocates of a smaller government, however, argue that any tax increase would reduce progress toward their ultimate goal of lower nondefense expenditures. They believe the deficits exert pressure for reduced spending. Recent history lends little support to this argument. The major cuts in nondefense programs were made in 1981 when the administration was not anticipating large budget deficits, and little has been done since then. In addition, the rise in the public debt and the cost of financing it has actually led to an expansion of government spending as a share of GNP. Moreover, the use of large deficits to exert pressure on nondefense spending has destroyed fiscal policy as a rational tool of overall economic stabilization policy, a development that threatens large costs for the private economy.

The Costs of Large Deficits and High Interest Rates

At present the Federal Reserve can afford to support a strong business expansion because the growth of demand raises little threat of increased inflation in an economy of 7 to 8 percent unemployment and capacity utilization rates of only 80 percent. However, as the economy begins to reach higher levels of resource utilization in the years after 1984, if the Federal Reserve is to avoid an acceleration of inflation it will be forced to restrict the supply of credit to offset the stimulus provided by the budget deficits. Thus today, and even more in the future, the mix of economic policy in the United States dictates high interest rates. High interest rates have serious consequences for domestic capital formation, the competitiveness of American industry in world markets, and the world economy, especially the economic position of less developed countries.

A projected budget deficit of 5 to 6 percent of GNP will absorb nearly two-thirds of net private savings in the United States, sharply curtailing the amount of resources available for domestic capital formation. The competition for private savings will drive up interest rates in the United States and attract foreign investors. The increased demand for dollars to invest in American capital markets will, in turn, increase the exchange rate.

Domestic Capital Formation. Since private saving has been a remarkably constant fraction of GNP over a long period, the rise in government dissaving seems likely to lower total national saving and reduce investment. This point is illustrated in table 2-5. Gross private saving (business plus individuals) inched up as a share of GNP throughout the postwar period, averaging 17 percent in the 1970s. While federal government deficits (dissaving) have fluctuated cyclically in prior decades, they

Table 2-5. *Saving and Investment as a Share of Gross and Net National Product, Selected Periods, 1951–89*

Item	Actual				Projected
	1951–60	1961–70	1971–80	1983	1986–89
	Percent of gross national product				
Gross national saving	**15.8**	**15.9**	**16.1**	**13.3**	**13.5**
Private	16.2	16.3	17.1	17.2	17.5
Federal government	−0.2	−0.5	−1.9	−5.5	−5.5
State and local government	−0.2	0.1	0.9	1.6	1.5
Plus: Net foreign capital inflow	**−0.3**	**−0.5**	**0.0**	**1.0**	**1.0**
Equals: Gross domestic investment	**15.6**	**15.4**	**16.1**	**14.2**	**14.5**
Nonresidential	10.4	11.1	11.5	10.3	10.5
Residential	5.2	4.3	4.6	3.9	4.0
	Percent of net national product				
Net national saving[a]	**7.6**	**8.1**	**6.9**	**2.1**	**3.0**
Private	8.0	8.6	8.0	6.6	7.5
Government	−0.4	−0.5	−1.1	−4.4	−4.5
Plus: Net foreign capital inflow	**−0.3**	**−0.5**	**0.0**	**1.2**	**1.0**
Equals: Net domestic investment[a]	**7.3**	**7.6**	**6.9**	**3.2**	**4.0**

Sources: U.S. Department of Commerce, Bureau of Economic Analysis, *The National Income and Product Accounts of the United States, 1929–74 Statistical Tables,* a supplement to the *Survey of Current Business* (GPO, 1977), and subsequent issues; and author's projections.

a. Net saving and investment equals the gross flow minus capital-consumption allowances (the depreciation of existing capital). Net national product equals gross national product minus capital-consumption allowances.

have averaged less than 2 percent of GNP over the course of most business cycles. The buildup of reserves of state and local employee pension funds has been a significant offset to a rising trend in the size of the federal deficit. As a result, national saving of about 16 percent of GNP has consistently been available to be divided among residential construction, business investment, and investment overseas. Throughout the postwar period, the United States has been a net creditor to the rest of the world, and income on foreign investments has been a major source of foreign exchange earnings.

This pattern is projected to change sharply over the 1980s under current budget policies. The sharp rise in the deficit must be offset by some combination of increased private saving, foreign capital inflows (a trade deficit), or reduced domestic investment. It was relatively easy to finance the deficit during the recession because the large overhang of excess capacity sharply curtailed business investment demand. In later stages of the recovery, however, rising investment demand will put added pressure on capital markets. The current strength of business investment and homebuilding in the face of interest rates of 10 to 13 percent suggests that future rates may have to soar to extremely high levels simply to hold the growth of demand within noninflationary limits.

In the projections shown in table 2-5 a small rise in private saving rates and some growth in the pension reserves of state and local governments provide for an increased rate of saving relative to the 1970s equal to about 1 percent of GNP. When the rise in the federal deficit of 3.5 percentage points is taken into account, the gross national saving rate is expected to fall by about 2½ percentage points. The United States must either curtail its rate of domestic investment or finance it through the inflow of capital from abroad. However, if domestic capital formation is maintained by foreign borrowing, the income from that capital will go abroad as well. Even if foreign capital inflows can be sustained at the current 1 percent of GNP there is little room for a recovery of capital formation from its recession levels: any gains in business investment as a share of GNP are likely to come at the expense of homebuilding.[11] The situation is even more alarming for net saving and investment (after deduction of the replacement investment required simply to offset depreciation of existing capital, currently about 11 percent of GNP). The net national saving rate will fall to less than half the average of the 1970s.

U.S. Competitiveness. From one perspective, the rise in the value of the dollar has been good news for American consumers: it has increased their purchasing power, and the reduction in prices of imported goods has been an important force behind the moderation of inflation. But it has been a disaster for workers and investors in export or import-competing industries. In effect, the rise in the value of the dollar has increased these industries' prices relative to those of their competitors in

11. It is possible that the foreign capital inflow could rise further, providing greater resources to finance some increase in domestic investment. Net foreign capital inflows equal to 2 percent or more of GNP in 1984–85 are projected by many private forecasts. But a trade deficit of that magnitude will be very difficult to maintain throughout the decade. It is also possible that private saving rates will rise more than projected; but there is little current evidence of such an increase despite an enormous rise in the after-tax return to private saving.

other countries by about 35 percent over the last three years. As a result, the United States has experienced an enormous decline in its net trade position with other countries, particularly in the areas of agriculture and capital equipment.[12]

Since the export industries tend to be the most innovative and efficient industries, there is also a cost to the economy as a whole in terms of a slower overall rate of innovation and growth. Furthermore, the overvalued dollar has not accelerated a necessary readjustment among the less efficient import-competing industries. Since rates of structural change that exceed normal rates of employee attrition impose very substantial costs on individuals and communities, they often perceive the problem as unfair foreign competition and seek trade protection.

While the public discussion of trade policies has focused on perceptions of unfair competition, there has been far too little recognition that the damage to the U.S. trade position caused by its own choice of a particular combination of fiscal and monetary policies is far greater than the harm wrought by foreigners. The deficit in the U.S. trade account is primarily a reflection of high interest rates and the imbalance between domestic saving and investment in the United States.

The World Economy. The appreciation of the dollar has had both positive and negative effects on other countries. It has clearly stimulated their exports. A weaker dollar would damage their competitive position in world markets, as it would enhance that of the United States. On the other hand, just as the high dollar has helped to reduce inflation in the United States, it has exacerbated inflation in other countries.

Some countries argue that they have been forced to adopt more restrictive monetary policies than they desire from a domestic perspective in order to match the high interest rates

12. The United States had a net international investment position of $168 billion ($834 billion of assets minus $666 billion in liabilities) at the end of 1982. That may understate the net asset position of the United States because it does not include revaluations of physical capital assets. Still, with projected annual current-account deficits near $75 billion annually, the United States should become a net debtor to the rest of the world in the latter half of the 1980s. It ill behooves the richest country in the world to be a net borrower, drawing scarce capital from other countries to finance its own budget deficits—particularly when its government officials lecture the least developed nations on the need to live within their means.

in the United States and thus prevent a fall in the value of their currencies. They also maintain that they are prevented from using expansionary monetary policies to raise their own economies out of the recession. Any country that acts in isolation to reduce its interest rates is likely to experience an immediate and substantial outflow of capital.

There is merit in these complaints, but they may overemphasize the importance of U.S. policies. Many of the industrialized countries have followed a perverse fiscal policy throughout the recession. Although their actual budget deficits have widened with the recession-induced loss of revenue and increased outlays for unemployment, their governments have enacted tax increases and expenditure reductions. Such actions by Japan and the major European countries have offset much of the stimulus to the world economy provided by fiscal expansion in the United States.[13] Thus, while a shift in the U.S. policy mix toward fiscal restraint and an easing of monetary policy would aid the world economy by reducing interest rates, significant gains would also follow from an opposite shift in the policy mix in other industrial countries.

The impact on developing countries is far more serious. The combination of the worldwide recession and the appreciation of the dollar resulted in a large fall in the prices of basic commodities and the exports of the developing countries. Their difficulties were exacerbated by the sharp acceleration of interest rates in the early 1980s. This forced them to devote an ever-increasing share of their reduced export earnings to meet interest and repayments on their external debt, much of which was denominated in U.S. dollars. The emergence of severe balance-of-payments difficulties within the largest of the borrowing countries has forced them to adopt restrictive domestic economic policies in an effort to reduce import requirements. These problems of debt financing are particularly serious in Latin America, the Philippines, and, to a lesser extent, Africa, where the growth in debt has been most dramatic.

---

13. Organization for Economic Cooperation and Development, *OECD Economic Outlook*, vol. 34 (December 1983), pp. 23–37.

Reasons for Acting Soon

The United States is indulging in a boom of public and private consumption financed by a liquidation of its net assets, both foreign and domestic. Future generations will experience a reduced standard of living—a smaller capital stock and the burden of repaying that foreign debt.

Moreover, there are reasons for acting quickly to reduce the deficit. First, the United States has had very little experience with a combination of such monetary and fiscal policy extremes, and the response of the economy to a sustained period of high interest rates is uncertain. The current policy mix increases the risk that a mistake in future monetary policies may precipitate an unintended recession (excessive restraint) or outburst of inflation (excessive accommodation).

Second, a continued rise in the public debt as a ratio to GNP, combined with high interest rates, requires ever-increasing tax rates simply to meet the interest payments. Each year that the United States postpones action on its deficit adds $200 billion to $300 billion to the debt and increases annual interest payments by $20 billion to $30 billion. That is a permanent cost to current and future generations.

Moreover, future planned changes in fiscal policy could be completely swamped by unforeseen changes in interest rates and thus expenditures. At the projected 1989 public debt of $2.6 trillion, a change in interest rates of as little as 1 percentage point would add $26 billion to the annual deficit. If a recession of average severity should occur during 1985–89, the budget deficit would rise into the range of $400 billion. In such a situation it would be very difficult to argue for additional fiscal stimulus as a countercyclical policy.

Finally, the problem of inadequate national saving will become more serious in the years after 1985. There are limits on the speed with which private investment can be expected to rise to offset the aggregate demand effects of a sharp shift in fiscal policy; but by adopting a deficit-reduction program that begins now and stretches over several years, Congress can reduce the risk that its own actions will precipitate a future recession.

Policy Options

A budget deficit growing to over $300 billion annually by the end of the decade may appear insuperable. If it were to be eliminated solely by raising taxes, it would require a tax increase of about $1,200 per capita, or nearly $5,000 annually for a family of four. Alternatively, it is equivalent to one-fourth of total expenditures. Fortunately, such a perspective overstates the magnitude of the problem if—but only if—the United States acts quickly to change its current monetary and budget policies. Much of the growth of the deficit is the result of the cumulative financing cost of the public debt. Prompt action to curtail the current deficit will yield large dividends in future years through additional interest savings. In addition, a change in the mix of the nation's fiscal and monetary policies, offsetting the depressive effects of fiscal restraint with an easing of monetary policy, can be expected to reduce interest rates and thus the cost of financing the existing debt.

There are two key elements of an effective program to cut future deficits: quick legislative action and the cooperation of the monetary authorities. Early action sharply reduces the magnitude of the required legislative actions. At current interest rates of 10 percent, because of the compound effect of interest financing, a $1 billion annual expenditure reduction would reduce the annual budget deficit after five years by a total of $1.7 billion—achieving $0.7 billion of additional savings in interest payments. Furthermore, a reduction in the deficit would contribute directly to lower interest rates by reducing federal borrowing in capital markets. Thus the actual savings would exceed $1.7 billion.

Cooperation of the monetary authorities is vital to sustain the growth of the economy in the face of any restrictive budget actions. A large and rapid decrease in the budget deficit would result in an excessive reduction of aggregate domestic demand and perhaps cause a recession. In order to see that the reduction in the budget deficit is offset by an increase in domestic

Table 2-6. *Proposed Budget Actions and the Deficit, Selected Fiscal Years, 1983–89*
Billions of dollars unless otherwise indicated

Item	1983	1985	1987	1989
Current services as projected by CBO	−195	−197	−245	−308
Percent of GNP	−6.1	−5.0	−5.3	−5.7
Legislative actions	0	40	120	200
Associated interest saving	0	12	43	88
Revised deficit	−195	−145	−82	−20
Percent of GNP	−6.1	−3.7	−1.8	−0.4

Source: Author's calculations as described in the text.

investment and net exports, it would be necessary to allow for a substantial decline in interest rates and the foreign exchange value of the dollar.

Fiscal Policy

At present, the major goal of Congress should be to develop a budget program that will restore national saving to its historical average of 16 percent by 1987. It is in that period that private demand for new capital can be expected to increase rapidly. If the legislative actions to reduce the budget deficit are sustained beyond 1987, the United States can expect to approach a balanced budget by the end of the decade. Such a program would provide the resources required for private investment during the recovery and relieve pressures on foreign borrowing.

A deficit-reduction program sufficient to restore the national saving rate of 16 percent of GNP by 1987 and make substantial progress toward achieving a budget balance by the end of the decade is outlined in table 2-6. Legislative actions (either tax increases or program expenditure reductions) that would reduce the deficit by $40 billion in 1985 and an additional $40 billion per year thereafter would result in a savings of $120 billion a year in fiscal year 1987 and $200 billion in fiscal year 1989.

Legislative action to reduce future budget deficits could also be expected to result in a substantial decline in market interest rates. That fall in interest rates and the resulting lower cost of financing the public debt would be a major source of future expenditure savings. The precise magnitude of the interest rate decline that would be associated with a shift in the mix of fiscal and monetary policies is highly uncertain, however. A reduction in the budget deficit equivalent to about 3 percent of GNP would restore the national saving rate to its historical postwar average. And a policy of balancing the budget by the end of the decade would raise the national saving rate significantly above the historical average. Those actions could be expected to reduce real interest rates to more normal levels. After several years of severe restraint, there would undoubtedly be considerable pent-up private demand which, together with a reversal of the previous capital inflows into the United States, would still keep interest rates relatively high. Memories of past inflation might also operate to keep investors' inflation expectations high in the future. On the other hand, if fiscal policy did shift substantially toward restraint, the monetary policy needed to maintain total demand would imply substantial short-term reductions in interest rates. On balance, it seems reasonable to anticipate that market interest rates would decline about 2 percentage points below the 4 percent real rate assumed by the CBO, and far below the current rate, in response to the proposed shift in the mix of fiscal and monetary policies.

The reduced size of the public debt and lower interest rates would save an additional $88 billion annually by 1989. The overall budget deficit would be less than 2 percent of GNP by fiscal year 1987, and below 1 percent by fiscal year 1989. Although market interest rates could decline by 2 percentage points beginning in 1985, this decline's initial effect on interest payments is limited by the lag in refinancing the debt with longer maturities. However, 90 percent of the debt is subject to refinancing by the end of the decade.

Annual adjustments of $40 billion are well within the range of fiscal policy adjustments that the economy could be expected to absorb without significant risk of precipitating a recession. They are, for example, smaller than the annual shifts in fiscal policy induced by the legislative actions taken in 1981 (see table 2-4). By 1989 cumulative savings on the public debt would amount to $850 billion and the ratio of debt to GNP would decline below the levels of fiscal year 1983.

Monetary Policy

The inconsistency between monetary and fiscal policies has been very costly to the U.S. economy in recent years. The conflict between a restrictive monetary policy aimed at slowing inflation and an expansionary fiscal policy has placed a heavy burden on those sectors of the U.S. economy most sensitive to interest rates and foreign competition.

In part, the imbalance of economic policy has resulted because the overall economic objectives of fiscal and monetary policy have been inconsistent with one another. Federal Reserve officials continue to emphasize restraint of inflation while remaining vague on their goals for real growth and unemployment. Meanwhile, the administration and Congress have stressed economic recovery as their primary objective. If the long-run issues of the budget deficit are to be resolved, the Federal Reserve must be prepared to allay the concern that restrictive budgetary actions will terminate the economic recovery.

A better balance of economic policy would result if the appropriate goal for overall growth of the economy (the clash between inflation and unemployment) could be clearly separated from the issue of the appropriate mix of fiscal and monetary policy to achieve that goal. With respect to the first issue, the economic projections that underlie the CBO budget estimates assume that between fiscal years 1983 and 1989 the growth of real GNP averages 3.9 percent annually and unemployment declines gradually to 6.5 percent. That is a modest pace of economic recovery that seems consistent with their projections of an inflation rate remaining in the range of 4 to 5 percent. As such, the projection should be acceptable to the Federal Reserve as a minimal goal consistent with their concerns about a future intensification of inflation pressures. Congress, the administration, and the Federal Reserve need to reach a consensus on a goal for overall growth, and the CBO projections would provide a reasonable basis from which to begin.

Initially, tax increases and expenditure reductions will tend to reduce the rate of economic growth. Thus it is vital that the monetary authorities be prepared to change their own policies so as to offset the depressive effect of the fiscal restraint and maintain a recovery along the agreed-upon path. They should not establish rigid targets for either interest rates or the money supply, emphasizing instead goals for real output and employment growth consistent with a nonacceleration of inflation. By doing so they can contribute to increasing domestic capital formation and restoring a balanced trade with the rest of the world.[14] Assurances that they are willing to take such measures to maintain a common target for overall economic growth will significantly improve the likelihood that the required budget actions will be taken.

Summary

Large budget deficits have been an important factor in the current recovery of the U.S. economy from recession. There are, however, substantial long-run costs to the United States and the world economy of continuing to maintain government spending far greater than tax revenues. Most of these problems arise out of the effort to combine a very expansionary fiscal policy that promotes higher levels of public and private consumption with a restrictive monetary policy that seeks to avoid an acceleration of inflation. The result has been a decline in national saving and investment and a large trade deficit with the rest of the world.

The economy would benefit substantially from a reversal of the current mix of economic policies. A reduction in the budget deficit would raise national saving, and an easier monetary policy would promote the pass-through of that saving into domestic capital formation. Reduced competition in domestic capital markets would lower interest rates, reduce foreign borrowing, and promote a decline in the foreign exchange rate

14. Some rise in inflation will be an unavoidable consequence of a decline in the exchange rate and a rise in import prices. As mentioned at the beginning of this chapter, the extreme rise in the exchange rate was one transitory factor that exaggerated the progress that the United States has made in recent years toward achieving a sustained reduction of inflation.

to a level that would allow U.S. industries to again compete on an equal footing in world markets.

Although there is a significant potential saving in interest on the public debt accompanying deficit reduction, the magnitude of the required legislative actions clearly indicates that a serious effort to reduce the deficit will require *both* expenditure reductions and tax increases. Specific suggestions in both of these areas are the subjects of the following chapters.

3

Reducing the Growth
of Domestic Spending

As INDICATED in the previous chapter, we believe there is a strong economic case for reducing the deficit and doing it soon. There is no painless way—either spending must be cut or taxes raised. Quick action will lessen the pain by avoiding some of the debt service costs that will arise if decisions are delayed.

The choice among different ways of bringing the deficit down, however, depends heavily on noneconomic value judgments about the desirable size of government and the appropriate mix of government activities. Indeed, the main argument between the president and Congress on deficit reduction has been not over whether the deficit ought to be reduced, but over whether defense or domestic spending should be cut and whether and when taxes should be raised.

We believe that as a practical matter a plan for substantially reducing the deficit is unlikely to command majority support in Congress or in the country unless it reflects a compromise that is seen as being evenhanded and as distributing the necessary sacrifice broadly among taxpayers and beneficiaries of government programs. A compromise will require many people to accept policies that they regard as less than the best. Some will feel that too much has been cut from domestic programs or defense, or that taxes should be raised further, while others will feel that the spending cuts have been too

Alice M. Rivlin and Louise B. Russell undertook primary responsibility for drafting this chapter. The section on agriculture was written in consultation with Fred H. Sanderson of Resources for the Future.

Table 3-1. *Outlays for Domestic Programs as a Percentage of Gross National Product, Selected Fiscal Years, 1962–89*

Program	Actual					Projected		
	1962	1970	1980	1983	1985	1987	1989	
Total	**7.7**	**9.9**	**14.9**	**15.0**	**13.6**	**13.2**	**12.8**	
Payments to individuals	**5.0**	**6.4**	**10.4**	**11.8**	**10.8**	**10.4**	**10.3**	
Social insurance	3.4	4.2	6.8	8.1	7.4	7.1	7.1	
Social security	2.6	3.1	4.6	5.3	4.9	4.7	4.6	
Medicare	. . .	0.6	1.3	1.6	1.8	1.9	2.1	
Unemployment	0.7	0.4	0.7	1.0	0.5	0.4	0.3	
Other general retirement and disability	0.1	0.1	0.2	0.2	0.2	0.1	0.1	
Means-tested payments	0.5	1.0	2.1	2.2	2.0	1.9	1.9	
SSI, AFDC, and other income security	0.4	0.4	0.7	0.7	0.6	0.5	0.5	
Medicaid	. . .	0.3	0.5	0.6	0.6	0.6	0.6	
Nutrition and housing assistance	0.1	0.2	0.8	0.9	0.7	0.7	0.7	
Student financial assistance	. . .	0.1	0.1	0.1	0.1	0.1	0.1	
Other	1.1	1.2	1.5	1.5	1.4	1.4	1.3	
Federal retirement	0.4	0.6	1.0	1.1	1.0	1.0	1.0	
Income security for veterans	0.7	0.6	0.5	0.4	0.4	0.4	0.3	
Other domestic programs	**2.7**	**3.5**	**4.5**	**3.2**	**2.8**	**2.8**	**2.5**	
Science, space, energy, natural resources, environment, and transportation	1.6	1.6	1.8	1.4	1.3	1.2	1.1	
Agriculture	0.7	0.5	0.2	0.7	0.4	0.4	0.4	
Community and regional development, education, training, employment, and social services	0.3	1.0	1.5	0.9	0.9	0.8	0.7	
Veterans' benefits and services (less income security)	0.3	0.3	0.4	0.3	0.3	0.3	0.2	
Other[a]	−0.2	0.1	0.6	−0.1	−0.1	0.1	0.1	

Sources: For 1962–83, Office of Management and Budget; projections, Congressional Budget Office. Figures are rounded.

a. Includes commerce and housing credit, civilian agency pay raises, offsetting receipts, health (less medicaid and medicare), administration of justice and general government, and general-purpose fiscal assistance.

small and the tax increases too large. Only if all groups are willing to make some concessions can the deficit be brought down. This chapter and the two following ones discuss the major elements of a compromise plan.

In this chapter, after discussing spending trends, we propose a two-stage plan for reducing domestic spending to help lower the deficit. Stage one involves a one-year modified freeze on domestic spending. This would mean omitting all cost-of-living increases in individual benefit programs for one year (unless inflation exceeded 5 percent), except for benefits specifically directed to low-income people. It would also mean holding funds appropriated for other domestic spending programs at the same dollar levels for one year.

Stage two involves more basic long-run restructuring of domestic spending. It emphasizes proposals to reduce the growth of benefits in social security, medicare, federal retirement programs, and agriculture.

Trends in Domestic Spending

In the 1960s and 1970s the federal government took on substantial new responsibilities and raised levels of spending for existing programs (see table 3-1). Spending for domestic programs rose from less than 8 percent of GNP in fiscal 1962 to about 15 percent in fiscal 1980. Much of this growth was in social insurance programs, such as social security, medicare, and unemployment compensation, which together accounted for about 7 percent of GNP in 1980. Growth also occurred in benefit payments for low-income people—welfare, food stamps, medicaid, and the like—which accounted for about 2 percent of GNP in 1980. A wide range of other domestic programs, such as aid for education, highways, and science, also grew in the 1960s and 1970s.

Growth in domestic spending as a percentage of GNP slowed dramatically in the early 1980s, when substantial cuts were made in many programs. On the basis of current policies, domestic spending as a percentage of GNP is projected to fall gradually to less than 13 percent by 1989.

Spending Increases, 1960–80

The social security program finances the benefits paid to retired people (and to survivors and the disabled) with a payroll tax levied on current workers. The programs' outlays grew in part because more and more people reached retirement age with enough years of coverage to qualify for benefits. By the early 1970s more than 90 percent of those who reached the age of sixty-five qualified for retirement benefits. Outlays also grew as Congress regularly increased the level of benefits more rapidly than rises in the cost of living. In 1972 Congress raised benefits 20 percent and—in an effort to hold down future increases—approved a new system under which, beginning in 1975, benefits would be raised automatically every year to reflect increases in the consumer price index.

The medicare program was enacted in 1965 to help pay the medical bills of people sixty-five or older; beginning in 1973, beneficiaries of social security's disability program and people needing kidney dialysis were also covered under the program. The largest part of the program—accounting for 70 percent of outlays—covers hospital care and, like social security, is financed by a payroll tax. Coverage of doctors' services is financed separately, in part by a premium paid by beneficiaries and in part by general revenues.

Along with private health insurance, medicaid, and other health programs, medicare has been an important element in the growth over the last several decades of third-party payment for medical services. Third-party payment has made it possible for doctors and hospitals to improve substantially the quantity and quality of services on the basis of medical criteria, without the need to worry about cost. Outlays for medicare—like other medical payments, both public and private—have grown steadily, largely because of the increasing number and sophistication of services associated with each episode of illness.

Outlays for means-tested programs, which are directed to the poor, grew between 1960 and 1980 chiefly because of the development of new programs. Food stamps, the largest of the nutrition assistance programs, began as an experiment in a few economically depressed areas in the early 1960s and had become a national program by 1970. The medicaid program was enacted in 1965, at the same time as medicare; it provides matching funds to the states so that they can pay for medical services for people on welfare, and sets guidelines for the operation of state programs. The number of people eligible for welfare and the percentage of those eligible who actually applied for it rose substantially in the years after the passage of medicaid, which contributed to increases in outlays for both welfare and medicaid. In 1972 Congress created the supplemental security income (SSI) program, which replaced the federal-state program of welfare for the elderly, blind, and disabled with a uniform national program of income benefits financed through general revenues; aid to families with dependent children (AFDC) remains a federal-state program. Programs of housing assistance were also developed during the 1960s and 1970s to assist low-income households with rent payments and to subsidize the construction of low-income housing. Grants and loans to students were greatly expanded.

The same period saw the creation of other new federal programs as well as the expansion of older ones. Grants to state and local governments were provided to improve the education of poor children at the preschool, elementary, and secondary levels. Other grants were for community development; for social services, such as day care and adoption services; for law enforcement; for mental health centers; and, under the general revenue-sharing program, for general support of state and local government. At the same time, growing public concern over the quality of the environment gave rise to new laws and a new agency, the Environmental Protection Agency, to administer them. The energy crisis of the 1970s generated new programs for energy research and conservation. Meanwhile, outlays for federal retirement benefits grew as an increasing number of federal employees reached retirement age and a mechanism was introduced to raise benefits automatically with increases in the cost of living.

Spending Cuts, 1981–83

Concern over the rapid growth of domestic spending developed in the 1970s. Some grants to state and local governments, held down in the late 1970s, failed to keep pace with inflation, but outlays for payments to individuals continued to grow in response to high inflation and rising unemployment.

In 1981 a break was made with the budgetary patterns of the past when President Reagan proposed, and Congress approved, a dramatic package of budgetary actions including defense spending increases, tax cuts over three years, and domestic spending reductions.

The first cuts were primarily in domestic spending programs that Congress controls directly through annual appropriations, especially in grants to state and local governments for manpower training, community development, and general purposes. Spending for these programs, labeled "other domestic programs" in table 3-1, dropped from 4.5 percent of GNP in 1980 to 3.2 percent in 1983. A major exception to the rule was agricultural outlays, which tripled as a share of GNP between 1980 and 1983 because of both new farm legislation passed in 1981 and two years of record crops and weak export markets.

Eligibility rules for means-tested entitlements were tightened to focus benefits on the poorest of the poor. The main result was that many of the working poor lost their eligibility for welfare payments, food stamps, medicaid, and other programs. Outlays for the large means-tested programs, such as welfare and food stamps, maintained their GNP share because the number of poor people grew during the recession, offsetting the effects of benefit reductions and tighter eligibility requirements. Federal matching funds for the medicaid program were trimmed, which slowed the growth in its share of GNP.

Social insurance programs largely escaped serious attention in the first round of domestic budget cutting, but the president and Congress were forced to address the social security program in 1983, when reserves in the social security trust fund were reaching dangerously low levels. Reserves had been drawn down by the impact of an unexpected combination of economic circumstances: high inflation, which increased indexed benefit payments, and slow economic growth, which reduced payroll tax collections below expected levels. If action was not taken to rebuild reserves, benefit checks could not go out on schedule. The social security amendments of 1983 included provisions to slow the growth in outlays and raise the revenues of the social security retirement program. The date for the annual cost-of-living adjustment in benefits was moved from June to December, beginning in 1983; this delay held benefits at June 1983 levels for six additional months. If the program's reserves fall below specified levels, the annual increase will be based on the increase in either prices or wages, whichever is lower, rather than simply on prices as in the past. For the longer term, expenditures are to be reduced by gradually moving the age at which a retiree can collect full benefits from sixty-five to sixty-seven, beginning in 2000. The same legislation reduced net benefits by subjecting a portion of benefits to federal personal income tax. It also included a new, prospective system for paying hospitals under medicare; medicare now pays a fixed rate, which depends on the condition of the patient, for each hospital stay.

Projected Changes, 1984–89

The Congressional Budget Office projects that domestic spending will decline from its high of 15 percent of GNP in 1983 to less than 13 percent by the end of the decade. Except for medicare, which is expected to continue to grow as a share of GNP, and medicaid, which will hold constant, all areas of domestic spending will share in the decline to some degree. The social insurance programs will fall the least; "other domestic programs" will fall the most.

In the effort to balance the budget by 1989, domestic spending must be reviewed again. The decision about whether to cut domestic spending and, if so, which programs should be reduced or eliminated involves political judgments. Because of their size (56 percent of anticipated federal domestic spending in 1989), social insurance programs cannot escape scrutiny, even though reductions were negotiated laboriously only last year. Some other programs, such as federal retirement and agriculture, invite attention because they are large or have grown rapidly.

The Short-Term Proposal: Stage One

It is important to begin to reduce the deficit quickly. Because a deficit-reduction plan will necessarily involve compromise, it should be evenhanded, spreading the spending cuts widely over many programs. For the short term, a plan for domestic programs that meets these criteria is a modified freeze on spending for fiscal 1985.

Under such a freeze, cost-of-living adjustments, up to a maximum of 5 percent, would be omitted in 1985. In programs like social security and the federal retirement systems that adjust benefits for inflation every year, adjustments would be omitted if prices rose less than 5 percent. If prices rose more than 5 percent, benefits would be adjusted upward by the difference between the actual rise in prices and 5 percent. Thus the beneficiaries of these programs would be protected against the possible resurgence of high rates of inflation.

The rates paid to hospitals by medicare under the new payment system (explained more fully in the next section) will be increased each October 1. The law does not specify, however, what rate of increase should be granted, other than to say that outlays should be no greater in fiscal 1985 than they would have been under the temporary system of rates included in the Tax Equity and Fiscal Responsibility Act of 1982. That legislation called for increases equal to the rate of increase in hospital input prices over the year, plus 1 percent for new services. This is the rate assumed in the CBO's projections of outlays. As part of the short-run freeze, the inflation part of the increase should be omitted (unless the index rises more than 5 percent) and only the 1 percent for new services allowed. This allowance would permit some flexibility for adjustments in a system that is still very new.

Physician fees under medicare should be held at 1984 levels, again unless the index being used exceeds 5 percent. In fairness to beneficiaries, whose incomes often depend importantly on social security benefits, the medicare cost-sharing amounts that are indexed to inflation should also be held at 1984 levels, subject to a reverse sort of cap: if inflation exceeds 5 percent, they should be increased by the difference.

Appropriations for programs that do not have automatic inflation adjustments should, as much as possible, be held constant at 1984 levels during the freeze. This will, of course, erode real spending levels by the amount of inflation.

Benefit payments directed specifically to low-income people should be exempted from the freeze. These include food stamps, aid to families with dependent children, supplemental security income, and housing assistance. These programs protect the poorest groups in society and have already been cut. Although outlays may decline naturally as economic recovery brings jobs and better income to some of the poor, further cuts in benefits per person would not be justified. Medicaid could be subject to continued limits on federal matching funds of the kind in effect during 1982–84.

The proposed freeze would save about $15 billion in 1985 if the CBO's most recent projection of the inflation rate (5.2 percent for fiscal 1985) is accurate. Since the one-year freeze would lower the base from which future increases are computed, saving would continue into the future. Indeed, saving in 1986 and beyond would be more than $20 billion annually: since the dates for many cost-of-living adjustments occur several months into the fiscal year, the full effect of the freeze would not be felt until the year after its enactment.

The Long-Term Proposal: Stage Two

Additional cuts in domestic spending must be considered as part of the effort to reduce the deficit further after 1985 and to contribute toward the goal of a budget surplus in the 1990s. These longer-term spending cuts should be based on a careful assessment and restructuring of domestic programs. This section suggests ways to restructure programs in four major areas of domestic spending: social security, medicare, federal retirement, and agriculture.

Programs for the poor are exempted from these proposals, as they were from the short-term freeze. Relieving poverty and helping people to move out of poverty are important functions of the federal government. The existing programs that serve those functions have already been cut substantially and should not be cut further. Indeed, we believe the federal government should improve its programs for the poor. In chapter 7 we discuss additional proposals to alleviate poverty.

Social Security

A few years ago the social security system was contributing to the federal budget deficit by paying out more in benefits than it was taking in in taxes, and drawing down its reserves. The 1983 social security amendments reversed this drain. The retirement and disability trust funds are now expected to run surpluses and to build up reserves to levels that would allow the system to weather another period of economic adversity comparable to that of the 1970s, should one occur again. Growth in total outlays for social security will continue at moderate rates until early in the next century, when the large generation born after World War II begins to retire.

It would be prudent to build up reserves in the late 1980s somewhat faster than now contemplated, but once a safe level of reserves is reached, there is little justification for running a social security surplus to finance other kinds of government expenditures. If reducing spending for social security is thought desirable, the payroll tax should be reduced commensurately. This would make it possible to raise other taxes to support spending in other areas without increasing the total federal tax burden.

Social security is the nation's basic retirement system. It provides a major portion of income for many retirees and is the only income for some. It thus serves as the first tier of benefits, available to nearly everyone, in a system of pension benefits that is supplemented by employer-sponsored pensions and individuals' own savings.

Picking the "right" level for the basic tier of retirement benefits involves weighing the importance of the basic benefit for the elderly against the other public and private needs of the nation. In view of the pressure likely to continue on the federal budget into the foreseeable future, we believe steps should be taken to reduce the automatic growth in social security spending moderately, to give the political system slightly more future flexibility in the choice between social security benefit increases and other federal activities. It is always easy to increase benefits above automatic levels; it is difficult to reduce them. Moderating built-in growth would increase future options.

Since the mid-1970s, social security retirement benefits have been designed to increase automatically in two ways:

—A worker's earnings history is indexed by the increases in average wages since the earnings were reported. A formula that is updated annually is then applied to these adjusted earnings to determine the worker's initial retirement benefit.[1] During normal times, when wages rise faster than prices, these adjustments mean that the initial benefit has been adjusted upward not only for the increase in the price level over the years but also for increases in productivity.

—Once the worker is retired, the initial benefit is adjusted for inflation each year to maintain its purchasing power.

Reductions in the automatic growth of social security outlays can be accomplished either by reducing cost-of-living increases or by changing the benefit formula in ways that lower the initial benefit for new retirees.

Because social security is the basic benefit for most people— and the only source of retirement income for some—we believe its purchasing power should be maintained during retirement. Retirement benefits should continue to be fully adjusted for inflation as specified in current law, with exceptions made only in extraordinary circumstances like those of the present. If benefits after retirement were normally indexed by something less than the cost of living, those who had been retired for a long time could find their benefits eroded to the vanishing point.

Thus we believe that further reductions in the automatic growth of outlays should be achieved through changes in the initial benefits. There are many ways to do this. A simple approach would be a permanent reduction in initial benefits by the percentage amount of the cost-of-living adjustment omitted during the short-term freeze. If the cost-of-living increase forgone in 1985 is 5 percent, for example, then the initial benefits of all future retirees would also be reduced by 5 percent. This approach would ensure that people retiring in

1. The initial benefit is equal to 90 percent of the first $267 (in 1984) of average monthly earnings, 32 percent of the next $1,345, and 15 percent of any earnings in excess of $1,612. The dollar amounts specified in the formula are updated every year by the rate of increase in average wages. The initial benefit is then increased to include any allowances for dependents or to conform, in certain cases, with special provisions of the law.

1986, just after the short-term freeze, would not have benefits much higher than those who had retired a year or two earlier and had been subject to the freeze.[2]

This approach would produce greater savings than under current law during the 1980s, when the deficit is expected to be acute, and would continue to produce savings beyond the decade. By about 2015, when virtually all beneficiaries would have retired under the changed system, outlays for retirement benefits would be 5 percent less than without the change.

An alternative approach, which would produce even greater savings over the long run, would involve indexing the dollar amounts specified in the benefit computation formula (the so-called bend points) by the increase in prices rather than wages. During normal times, when wages rise faster than prices, this would mean that the bend points would rise more slowly than under the current system, and, as a result, so would initial benefits. Replacement rates would gradually follow a new pattern: instead of receiving a higher real benefit for a given real wage, each succeeding generation of retirees would receive the same real benefit.

Savings would be small in the first few years but would gradually rise to be much larger than those under the first approach. The change would slowly move the automatic growth in outlays—the growth that occurs because of the indexation built into the formula—to a level substantially lower than that projected for the current system. Benefits, and outlays, could be left at this lower level, or discretionary increases could be added when Congress judged that economic and fiscal conditions could support them. If the future is like the past, and wages rise faster than prices most of the time, this change would give the government more flexibility to adjust spending to the conditions and values of the time than would the first approach.

Such flexibility would disappear, however, if the future

2. On the other hand, a short-term freeze is sometimes justified by the argument that social security benefits were overadjusted for inflation during the years 1979–82 because the consumer price index, which is used to make the adjustment, overstated inflation. New retirees did not benefit from that overadjustment, so there is no corresponding argument for reducing their benefits.

turned out to be more like the very recent past, with prices rising faster than wages. In that event, benefits and outlays would rise faster than under the current system. This problem would be relieved, but not removed, by the provision included in the 1983 social security amendments that will base the cost-of-living increase in benefits on the lower of wages or prices when the program's reserves fall below a certain level.

Together with the one-year freeze on benefits included in the short-term program, either of the two approaches would allow the social security trust fund to build up to safe levels faster than under current law. Thus it might be possible to reduce or omit the payroll tax increases scheduled for 1988 and 1990, and eventually to lower the tax rate, offsetting in part the increases in other taxes necessary to finance federal programs and easing the total federal tax burden.

Medicare and Medicaid

Congress recently enacted a prospective payment plan for hospitals to replace the previous system, under which medicare paid hospitals on the basis of their actual costs. Under the new plan medicare pays fixed rates per admission and the rates are set in advance of the year to which they apply. To reflect differences in the costs of caring for patients with different problems, separate rates are specified for each of 468 "diagnosis-related groups." The rate is the same for every patient in a given group, regardless of the services provided or the length of stay, and must be accepted as payment in full for the cost of inpatient care, except capital costs and costs associated with medical education. Hospitals whose costs are less than the rate can keep the difference; those whose costs are greater must absorb the loss.

The current law stipulates that the rates are to be increased every October. We propose that after the short-term freeze the annual increase in the rates be held to no more than inflation plus 1 percent. This policy represents a significant restraint on the growth of costs; between 1970 and 1982 costs per admission grew on average by 3.2 percent more than inflation each year.[3]

3. Inflation in the prices of hospital inputs ran somewhat ahead of general inflation.

The proposed policy would allow an increase of 1 percent for new services—more if improvements in productivity offset some of the increase in prices. Given the newness of the system and the effect of the short-term freeze on rates during 1985, it seems undesirable to try to impose a greater degree of restraint over the next few years.

This policy would produce additional savings in the years after the short-term freeze, but it would not contribute to reducing the budget deficits projected by the Congressional Budget Office, because those are already based on the assumption that the prospective rates will be allowed to rise only by inflation plus 1 percent each year. Even this degree of restraint will leave the medicare trust fund with a substantial deficit in the mid-1990s.[4]

To restore the medicare trust fund to solvency, it will be necessary either to increase the revenues flowing into the fund or to reduce outlays further, or some combination of the two. One approach to reducing outlays might be to shift medicare in the direction of major medical coverage for the elderly, which would require more cost sharing for small bills than under the present medicare program, but would provide better protection against large ones.

The medicaid program, which helps pay for medical services for the poor of all ages, has experienced financial strain not only from the rise in hospital costs but also from the rise in the demand for and cost of nursing home care. During the current budget crisis, medicaid should continue to be subject to the kinds of limits on federal matching funds that were in effect during 1982–84. Over the longer term, however, a good case exists for spending more on a medical program for the poor: the current medicaid program covers only some of the poor, and the level of coverage varies greatly among the states.

Federal Retirement

Like many private-sector employers, the federal government provides pension benefits for its retired employees. The civil

4. The CBO projects that the medicare trust fund's cumulative deficit will be nearly $100 billion by 1995.

service and military retirement plans are more generous than those available to employees in the private sector: initial benefits are higher; federal employees can retire with full benefits at younger ages than private-sector employees; and unlike the benefits from private pensions, which are only partially indexed if they are indexed at all, federal retirement benefits are fully indexed for inflation once the employee retires.[5]

In the private sector, employer pension plans are typically designed to supplement social security benefits. But civilian workers of the federal government were not covered by social security until recently. Beginning in 1984, *new* employees will be covered by social security, though few of them, of course, will be retiring in the next couple of decades. Members of the armed forces have been covered by social security for years.

For both military and civilian workers, however, total federal benefits are more generous than the combination of social security and the typical private-sector retirement plan. Full indexing of benefits has been especially beneficial to federal employees in the recent period of high inflation. Indeed, since federal wages and salaries, like those of the private sector, lagged behind prices in the late 1970s and early 1980s, federal employees who retired a decade or so ago have sometimes been more generously treated than those now in the work force.

Under the civil service system, an employee who has worked for the government for thirty years can retire with immediate benefits at age fifty-five. Under the military system, a service member is eligible for immediate benefits on completing twenty years of service. The civil service system is more generous to employees who have worked for the federal government for a long time than to shorter-term employees. It is also more generous to those who retire directly from the federal government than to those who leave to work elsewhere before retiring, because the earnings on which benefits are based are not indexed for inflation. The military system draws an even sharper distinction between short- and long-term employees:

5. These cost-of-living increases have, however, been delayed or capped several times in recent years, because of special exceptions made by Congress in its efforts to reduce spending.

servicemen who leave before completing twenty years of service receive nothing, while those who retire after twenty years or more receive a pension based on pay and years of service. The result is an odd system of incentives that may bear little relation to military manpower requirements. The pension system offers little inducement to reenlist after only a few years of service, big inducements for those getting close to the twenty-year mark, and little additional incentive after that.

In the past, generous federal retirement benefits have served several special functions. When federal pay was lagging behind pay in the private sector, they helped to retain federal workers by making total compensation (including fringe benefits) more comparable to that in the private sector. In the civil service generous retirement benefits have been used during the last decade to help reduce the federal work force by encouraging employees to retire early. In the military such benefits have been supported on the ground that, by encouraging retirement after twenty years, they keep the military forces relatively young and open up promotion opportunities for those who remain.

Not all these reasons are as valid as they once were. For the most part, civil service and military salaries are now reasonably competitive with salaries in the private sector, so there is less justification for retirement benefits that are more generous. Further, as the armed services use more technologically sophisticated equipment and methods, experience and skill become more valuable; it is no longer desirable to encourage experienced specialists and technicians to leave after twenty years. Changing conditions, as well as the size of the federal deficit, indicate that reductions in retirement benefits are advisable.

Reasonable changes to consider include reducing initial benefits somewhat and making full benefits available only at somewhat older ages than currently. With new federal employees now covered by social security, both the civil service and military systems can be designed to serve as the second tier of benefits in a pension program, as private-sector benefits do. Though we believe social security benefits should be fully indexed, we see less reason for full indexing of second-tier pensions, which meet less essential needs. Indeed, most private pensions are not fully indexed. Partial indexing of federal retirement benefits would help to slow the growth in outlays and would provide greater equity between private and public employees and between working people and retirees.

The CBO has estimated the savings from a new retirement plan for the civil service that includes these features—somewhat lower initial benefits, full benefits only at age sixty-two, and partial indexing for inflation (50 percent for benefits above $1,000 per month in 1984 dollars). Additional outlays of $500 million would be required in the first year, because employee contributions would be reduced, but savings would rise thereafter to almost $1 billion by the fifth year. These estimates indicate the magnitude of the savings that could be expected from a reasonable reform proposal.

Over the years commissions, the Defense Department's quadrennial review panels, and other advisory groups have made many proposals for reforming the military retirement system. Most of the proposals integrate military pensions with social security, reducing initial benefits for retirees under the age of sixty or sixty-two and vesting some benefits for those with ten to nineteen years of service; often the vesting would entitle the retiree to an old-age annuity but not to an immediate pension. Most of these advisory groups have also proposed less-than-full indexing for at least some benefits—sometimes only those received by retirees under sixty-two, with a catch-up adjustment when the retiree reaches sixty-two. We agree with these general principles and believe, in addition, that partial indexing should apply to all retirees, with a catch-up adjustment at age sixty-two.

Because so many proposals exist and the differences between them are often minor, we do not suggest a specific proposal. Any reform should have the characteristics just described. Any variant of these could produce substantial savings rather quickly. The CBO has estimated the savings for several reforms, including a synthesis plan that has most of the elements listed above, but not partial indexing for retirees sixty-two or older. It estimates that such a plan would save about $1 billion in 1989. This seems a reasonable amount to expect from a new plan, and the savings might be somewhat higher with partial indexing for those sixty-two or older.

Agriculture

Current agricultural programs are intended to serve several purposes: to yield farmers somewhat better returns on their labor and investment than the market alone would give them, and to reduce fluctuations in food supplies and prices and in farm incomes. The major programs cover wheat, feed grains, rice, soybeans, and upland cotton.[6] Because the higher-than-market returns tend to give farmers an incentive to produce more than the market can absorb, the programs try to offset these incentives with restraints on production. To qualify for federal benefits, grain and cotton farmers can be required to idle some of their land, and the government may pay them, in cash or in kind, for further, voluntary reductions in acreage. A farmer who chooses to meet the required acreage reductions is eligible for the following:

—Nonrecourse loans. The farmer may put his crops in storage and take a nine- to twelve-month loan from the government at a specified loan rate, or "support price"; interest is charged at the cost of money to the Treasury. If the farmer chooses not to sell his crop at the end of the loan period, because market prices are still too low, he keeps the loan and the government accepts the crop as payment.

—Farmer-owned grain reserve. Wheat and feed grain farmers may also enter into a contract with the Commodity Credit Corporation to put their crops into a farmer-owned reserve in return for an interest-free, three-year loan from the government. As long as the market price remains below a specified release level, the government pays the cost of storage and the farmer cannot take the grain out of storage unless he pays a penalty. If the market price rises above the release level, storage subsidies

6. These programs account for the bulk of agricultural outlays. There are somewhat different programs for other commodities; the most important of these is the dairy program, which has given rise to net outlays of over $2 billion in recent years. In addition, both the dairy and sugar programs rely on import protection, which imposes substantial costs on the American consumer.

cease and the farmer is charged interest, but he is free to sell the grain.

—Deficiency payments. When the market price, averaged over several months, is below a specified target price (which is higher than the support price), the farmer can qualify for a deficiency payment when he sells his crop. The payment is based on the farmer's average production, times the difference between the target price and the market price, or the support price (the nonrecourse loan rate), whichever is smaller. Deficiency payments are not available for soybeans.

Under the legislation and market conditions of recent years, the farm programs have become expensive. Total federal outlays for agriculture rose to $22 billion in fiscal 1983, up from $5 billion in fiscal 1980.[7] Although outlays are expected to drop in 1984 as market prices strengthen in the wake of the large reduction in feed grain and cotton stocks in 1983, they are projected to remain above the levels of the 1970s during the rest of the decade unless changes are made when the farm legislation comes up for renewal in 1985.

Despite the high cost, the programs have had little success in stabilizing markets in recent years. With their heavy dependence on exports, U.S. farmers have become increasingly vulnerable to international developments beyond their control, ranging from weather in distant places to farm and trade policies in other countries. Recent U.S. macroeconomic policies have been especially hard on farmers. High interest rates have raised their costs, and high values of the dollar have made U.S. agricultural exports less attractive to buyers. Moreover, in some ways U.S. farm programs have been damaging to exports. By restricting supplies and raising prices, the programs have encouraged production in competing countries and reduced the domestic market by making substitutes more attractive (for example, synthetic fibers for cotton).

The agriculture programs are not well designed to help the farmers who are most in need of help. Because payments are based on the quantities produced, large farms are the principal

7. In addition to the commodity programs, the total includes crop insurance, agricultural credit, and agricultural research and services, which amounted to $3.3 billion in 1983.

beneficiaries—the 12 percent of farms with sales over $100,000 account for two-thirds of total sales and over half of total federal payments.

We suggest that the new legislation take market stabilization as its primary goal, but that it should not attempt to raise prices above long-term market-clearing levels. Deficiency payments should be eliminated for all crops as they have been for soybeans. As is the case for soybeans, the nonrecourse loan rate, which would continue to act as a support price, might be set at 75 percent of the average market price over the three preceding years. With support prices below long-term market-clearing levels, it would be less expensive to induce farmers to participate in the grain reserve. Production should adjust to market demand and there should be no excessive buildup of government-owned or government-controlled stocks; consequently, there should no longer be a need for acreage reduction programs. If income supplements are needed by some farmers, they should be more precisely targeted to those in need.

The Congressional Budget Office has estimated budget savings from these changes would amount to more than $7 billion in 1986. They are projected to rise to more than $13 billion in 1989.

Other Domestic Programs

Although opportunities for large savings in programs other than those mentioned here are limited, we believe that a careful review of the whole range of domestic programs would yield many proposals that, taken together, would contribute both to the reduction of the federal deficit and to the more effective use of national resources. A reasonable goal for such a deficit reduction would be a total of $6 billion during 1986–89.

In any such review, emphasis should be given to increasing user fees if the service being provided benefits identifiable users. Many such services are now provided by the federal government without charge or at fees well below the federal cost. Such underpricing of government services may lead to uneconomic use of government resources. For example, the government pays for the maintenance of deep-water ports and harbors but does not charge commercial shippers for using them. Similarly, the use of federally maintained canals was free until 1981, and the fuel tax introduced in that year is expected to cover only about 10 percent of the federal costs of building, maintaining, and operating the canal system for the rest of the decade. These programs lead to uneconomic projects, ones that commercial users of ports and waterways would not support if they had to pay the cost. Higher user fees would produce some budgetary saving and help to discourage uneconomic new projects.

Further savings could be achieved by cutting the size of the federal subsidies for some activities or by reducing or eliminating some programs. For example, the federal government subsidizes mass transit systems generously, although the benefits are primarily local. Federal subsidies are best reserved for benefits that extend beyond local jurisdictions. In addition, programs such as general revenue sharing and community development block grants distribute funds for unrestricted, or very loosely restricted, purposes and were initiated at a time when the federal government was better able to raise revenues than were state or local governments. Now that budgetary conditions have changed, programs like these should be reconsidered.

Summary

This chapter proposes a two-part program to begin reducing domestic spending quickly and to restrain its growth over the longer run so that the budget can be brought into balance by the end of the decade. The modified freeze proposed for 1985 would save $15 billion in the first year and would give Congress time to put together a compromise plan that would make longer-run changes. The freeze would continue to contribute savings of more than $20 billion each year during 1986–89. The chapter discusses elements of a longer-run plan—possible changes in social security, medicare, federal retirement, agriculture, and other domestic programs—that would help to reduce the deficit further.

4

Paying for National Security

As PREVIOUS chapters have made clear, we believe high priority should be given to reducing the federal deficit by cutting outlays and raising revenues. Because defense outlays account for about 30 percent of all federal spending and are rising faster than other spending, they are an obvious source of possible deficit reductions.

Reducing the deficit at the expense of endangering national security, however, would be irresponsible. If we were convinced that the rapid defense buildup advocated by the Reagan administration were necessary to deter attack or deal effectively with threats to U.S. security, we would urge that it be continued and that its impact on the deficit be offset by higher taxes or cuts in other spending. We believe, however, that the pace of the administration's defense buildup, especially the remarkable increase in procurement, is both unjustified and unwise. A more moderate and balanced growth could meet the administration's defense objectives more efficiently. Indeed, forces appropriate to an even higher level of perceived threat and a need for more immediate readiness could be purchased for fewer dollars than the administration is proposing to spend.

After a brief discussion of trends in defense spending, this chapter focuses on the administration's five-year defense program for fiscal years 1985–89. It points out instances in which

William W. Kaufmann provided the background study for this chapter. A more complete and detailed discussion can be found in his *The 1985 Defense Budget* (Brookings Institution, forthcoming).

we believe the program is duplicative, is based on a weak rationale, or reflects an imprudent investment strategy. The chapter then suggests an alternative "efficient Reagan defense budget," a less expensive way of attaining essentially the same defense capability as that sought by the administration. Finally, the chapter discusses alternative budgets adapted to both greater and lesser levels of perceived threat to U.S. security.

Defense Spending: Past and Proposed

During much of the 1970s, when domestic spending by the federal government was growing more rapidly than GNP, defense spending as a percentage of GNP was declining. Defense outlays, which were about 8 percent of GNP in 1970 when the United States was still heavily involved in Vietnam, declined to about 5 percent before the Carter administration reversed the trend by undertaking a major modernization program for both nuclear and conventional forces. Moderni-

Table 4-1. *Changes in Defense Appropriations,*
Fiscal Years 1981–84
Billions of dollars unless otherwise specified

Appropriation account	1981[a]	1984	Real increase[b] (percent)
Military personnel	36.7	48.6	9.8
Retired military pay	13.8	16.6	4.9
Operation and maintenance	54.2	70.9	18.7
Procurement	45.0	86.0	59.6
Research, development, test, and evaluation	16.1	26.9	44.2
Military construction	3.4	4.5	15.1
Family housing and homeowners' assistance	2.0	2.7	18.4
Revolving and management funds	0.1	2.5	[c]
Financing adjustments	−1.0	−0.5	[c]
Budget authority	170.3	258.2	30.8
Outlays	157.6	231.0	24.4

Sources: *Department of Defense Annual Report, Fiscal Year 1982,* p. A-1; *Department of Defense Annual Report to the Congress, Fiscal Year 1985,* p. 279.
a. Budget as passed by Congress, but before amendment by President Reagan in 1981.
b. Nominal increase from previous year minus inflation.
c. The deflator for this category is unavailable.

Table 4-2. *The Reagan Defense Budget, Fiscal Years 1985–89*

Item	1985	1986	1987	1988	1989	Total
Budget authority						
Billions of dollars	305.0	349.6	379.2	411.5	446.1	1,891.4
Percent real increase[a]	13.0	9.2	3.5	3.8	3.9	21.9
Outlays						
Billions of dollars	264.4	301.8	339.2	369.8	398.8	1,674.0
Percent real increase[a]	9.3	8.4	7.0	4.1	3.3	24.9
Pay and price deflators	100.0	105.3	110.6	115.8	120.9	. . .

Source: *Department of Defense Annual Report, Fiscal Year 1985*, p. 71.
a. Nominal increase from the previous year minus inflation.

zation has been substantially accelerated by the Reagan administration. Defense outlays, about 6.5 percent of GNP in 1984, are projected to rise to about 7.3 percent of GNP by 1989.

Strengthening U.S. military forces has been the primary commitment of the Reagan administration's security policy, and increases in the defense budget have been the primary means for accomplishing that purpose. Measured against the last full budget of the Carter administration, defense budget authority has grown by 52 percent during President Ronald Reagan's first three years in office, or about 31 percent after allowance for inflation (see table 4-1). The original budget and the five-year defense plan submitted to Congress called for $305 billion in budget authority in fiscal year 1985 and increases to $446 billion by fiscal year 1989 (see table 4-2). The 1989 figure would represent a 22 percent real (inflation-adjusted) increase over the funds appropriated by Congress for military purposes in fiscal year 1984. Sustained increases of this magnitude are historically unprecedented in peacetime and certainly represent a dramatic manifestation of the president's commitment.

Under pressure from the Congress, the president agreed to revise his fiscal year 1985 defense budget and the next two years of his 1985–89 defense plan only a few weeks after submitting them. Defense budget authority in fiscal year 1985 under the revised plan would be reduced from $305 billion to $291 billion, and a total of $57 billion would be cut from budget authority in fiscal years 1985–87. Instead of a 13 percent real increase in appropriations from fiscal 1984 to fiscal 1985, the president accepted a 7.8 percent real increase. These conces-

sions have adjusted the timing but not the major outlines of
the administration's defense program.

The Reagan Program: An Investment Strategy

The administration's defense plan has been primarily a capital
investment program that puts extraordinary emphasis on upgrading the equipment of the armed forces. As table 4-1 shows,
the investment accounts—procurement, research and development, and military construction—have increased much faster
than other parts of the defense budget. Procurement alone
rose almost 60 percent after inflation between 1981 and 1984.
Increases in the accounts that reflect immediate operation of
the forces—pay or operation and maintenance, for instance—
have been far more modest. This disparity is scheduled to
continue under the administration's five-year plan.

With the ratio between spending for investment and for
immediate operations rising dramatically, unusual problems in
the management of defense resources are beginning to appear.
Because of the rate at which defense appropriations have grown
and because so many resources have gone to procurement, a
large and increasing backlog of budget authority either already
obligated or awaiting commitment to contracts has been created
(see table 4-3). This backlog will complicate any future effort
to control the growth of the defense budget in an orderly way.
Indeed, the backlog will account for about $94 billion of the
fiscal year 1985 budget outlays. If Congress holds the fiscal
1985 defense budget authority to about $290 billion, expendi-
tures from the backlog will come to more than $110 billion by
fiscal 1986. This will mean that at least 36 percent of defense

Table 4-3. *Growth in the Backlog of Defense Budget Authority
at the End of Each Fiscal Year, Fiscal Years 1981–85*
Billions of dollars

Item	1981	1982	1983	1984	1985
Obligated authority	86.3	107.6	128.7	155.4	188.4
Unobligated authority	26.5	34.6	43.4	43.0	50.5
Total	112.8	142.2	172.1	198.4	238.9

Sources: *Budget of the United States Government, Fiscal Year 1983*, p. 9-9; *Fiscal Year 1984*, p. 9-11; *Fiscal Year 1985*,
p. 9-16.

outlays will be committed and uncontrollable even before Congress takes action on the budget for that year. Because much of the rest of the defense budget, especially pay, cannot be realistically altered in the short run, room for future reductions in spending will be extremely limited.

Moreover, because the armed services are undergoing rapid, comprehensive, and simultaneous modernization, in about twenty years a new administration will have to decide what to do about all the tracked vehicles, ships, missiles, and aircraft that were acquired in such haste and are wearing out at roughly the same time. Even in the nearer term, difficult choices may emerge. Despite the introduction of decidedly more complex weapons systems, defense planners apparently expect to enter an era in which equipment malfunction and repair rates will actually decline, even though experience suggests otherwise. Eventually, Congress may have to choose between sustaining high defense budgets simply in order to operate, support, and modernize these costly capital goods or, if the rate of growth in defense spending is to be slowed, taking such draconian measures as reducing the readiness of the combat forces and mothballing modern equipment.

Basis for Reductions

We believe that defense budget authority for fiscal year 1985 can be brought down to about $260 billion and that future budgets can be held well below the levels planned by the administration while still maintaining all conditions essential to U.S. security. These reductions are possible for two reasons. First, it is now evident that when it came into office in 1981 the administration seriously misjudged what needed to be done to strengthen U.S. defenses. Second, lack of discipline in the Department of Defense planning process has led to duplications in weapons systems, an imprudent pace of investment, and pursuit of questionable objectives.

Initial Misjudgment

The Reagan administration's costly rush to modernize military equipment apparently reflects two beliefs: that the investment portion of the defense budget was badly neglected during the decade before the administration came to office and that the Soviet Union has been engaging in a rapid and massive modernization of its own nuclear and nonnuclear forces. Both beliefs are open to doubt. It is generally forgotten that U.S. ground forces and tactical air forces experienced considerable turnover of equipment during the war in Southeast Asia and ended that war with large stocks of modern weapons and supplies. U.S. naval forces did not experience a similar turnover, but they have been receiving new ships at an average rate of fourteen a year for nearly a decade. As for the Russians, the latest estimates from the Central Intelligence Agency indicate their defense spending has slowed from an average of 4 percent real growth per year in 1964–75 to about 2 percent per year in 1976–81.[1] Indeed, instead of engaging in the relentless buildup originally cited by the Reagan administration, the Soviets appear to have been replacing their capital stock at quite normal rates, considering the average service life of military equipment and the higher cost of the current generation of weapons.

Although many spokesmen talked early in the administration of the need to be able to fight a protracted nuclear war and a lengthy worldwide conventional conflict, in fact the administration has not been able to translate these goals into programs. Indeed, as these goals have seemed to recede, the administration has, for all practical purposes, settled for the basic strategy (but not the programs) established by Presidents Richard M. Nixon and Gerald R. Ford in the mid-1970s.

Despite the growth in allocations for defense, the country will achieve what is essentially a more modern and somewhat more sustainable version of the same military posture it settled for in 1975 in the wake of the Vietnam War. In effect, the defense planning process is producing a strategic nuclear force capable of delivering between 3,000 and 4,000 nuclear warheads on a retaliatory strike to targets in the Soviet Union. The planning process is also developing conventional forces able

---

1. *The Allocation of Resources in the Soviet Union and China—1983,* Hearings before the Subcommittee on International Trade, Finance and Security Economics of the Joint Economic Committee, 98 Cong. 1 sess. (Government Printing Office, forthcoming).

(but only with ample warning and in conjunction with allies that are less well equipped and supplied) to defend against the expected threats to Western Europe, the Persian Gulf states, and South Korea. The surge in investment has been concentrated almost entirely on weapons modernization; there have been no major changes in force structure. The capability of the force is being increased, albeit not at anything close to the rate of increase in expenditure. But the current force does not seem inappropriate if, as the administration apparently assumes, the international environment remains about as it now is: subject to small-scale tremors, as in the Middle East and Central America, but not in danger of major earthquakes despite the continued slow growth in the Soviet military establishment. If anyone believed that major conflict was an imminent possibility, however, it would be far more appropriate to concentrate on creating a larger force more ready for immediate action.

Undisciplined Planning

A second reason for further reductions in the defense budget grows out of current management practices in the Defense Department. The planning and programming reforms instituted in the Office of the Secretary in the 1960s and partly reinstituted in the 1970s have been abandoned. Programmatic and budgeting initiative has reverted to the three military services, which, freed from central direction and discipline, have behaved predictably. They have simply reviewed their traditional lists of priorities and asked for programs and funding denied them by previous administrations. Each has tried to contract for as much procurement as possible and has attempted to accelerate the pace of procurement before the budgetary feast once again turns into a relative famine. Each has been willing to accept considerable technological risk in order to get programs started and funded. Each has begun preparations to fight its own war independently of the other two. For lack of more than the most general guidance as to directions and resource constraints, each has also tried to plan in the 1980s just as it did in the 1970s, except that it has not had to be as selective and discriminating about investment policies.

The programmatic and budgetary consequences have been as predictable as this behavior. Investment accounts have burgeoned, as has duplication within and among the services. New weapons of questionable performance have gone into production, no doubt in the expectation that funds to make them more effective will be forthcoming once they are in the inventory. At the same time, older weapons, which are already in the field and performing the same functions as the new ones, are being upgraded. Efforts are being made to replace existing equipment before the end of its useful service life on the excuse that the USSR is making rapid technological progress, even though the evidence for that progress is rarely forthcoming. In response to generous increases in funding and nebulous proposals for changing U.S. strategy, some programs worthy at best of research and exploratory development are being pushed as though their performance and cost were well understood. Others, such as the 600-ship Navy, are being advanced as though they were unquestioned national objectives.

Savings that can be achieved by reverting to a more gradual and discriminating policy of modernization are discussed below. These savings do not result from challenges to detailed military assessments of particular weapons or to basic national strategy. Nor do they arise from a belief that reduction of the deficit requires a "fair" contribution from defense. Rather, they come from an attempt to accomplish three objectives: to reduce the amount of duplication in the five-year program, to slow the pace of replacement to levels appropriate for a normal turnover of the weapons inventory, and to eliminate capabilities that support questionable objectives.

Reducing Duplication

Examples of duplication abound in both strategic nuclear forces and general-purpose forces. Reducing duplication could save about $23 billion in fiscal year 1985 and more in subsequent years. Redundant programs that could be reduced or canceled are shown in table 4-4 and discussed briefly below.

Table 4-4. *Savings from Reduction of Program Duplication, Fiscal Year 1985*
Billions of dollars of budget authority

Program	Action	Savings
Strategic nuclear weapons		
B-1B bomber	Cancel	8.2
MX missile (Peacekeeper)	Cancel	5.0
Tactical nuclear weapons		
Tomahawk cruise missile (TLAM-N)	Reduce by 50 percent	0.3
Ground force weapons		
Copperhead artillery projectile	Cancel	0.1
Division air defense gun (Sergeant York)	Cancel	0.6
Patriot air defense missile	Cancel	1.3
AH-64 attack helicopter (Apache)	Cancel	1.5
Joint tactical missile system (JTACMs)	Reduce by 50 percent	0.1
Air Force and Navy aircraft		
F-15 fighter-attack aircraft	Cancel	2.3
Imaging infrared air-to-ground missile (IIR Maverick)	Cancel	0.6
AV-8B vertical takeoff and landing aircraft	Cancel	1.0
F-14A fighter aircraft	Cancel	1.0
F-14D fighter aircraft	Cancel	0.3
Phoenix air-to-air missile	Cancel	0.5
A-6E attack aircraft	Cancel	0.3
Sparrow air-to-air missile	Cancel	0.3
LAMPS I antisubmarine warfare helicopter	Cancel	0.1
Total savings	. . .	23.4

Sources: *Department of Defense Annual Report, Fiscal Year 1985*, pp. 113–202; and author's estimates. Numbers are rounded.

Strategic Nuclear Forces

Defense planners generally agree that U.S. strategic nuclear forces should be capable of a "countervailing strategy," that is, the ability on a retaliatory strike to hold in reserve a force for attacking cities and, with other offensive forces, to thwart any effort by an enemy to exploit the advantage of a nuclear attack. The destruction of a relatively small number of nonurban targets, principally nuclear and nonnuclear military bases, transportation links, and power plants, would ensure that the enemy had no chance of terminating the exchange to his long-term advantage and that he would pay an exorbitant price for trying.

The United States has such a force now, a combination of long-range bombers and land- and submarine-based missiles capable of delivering more than 3,700 warheads on a retaliatory strike to a wide range of targets in the Soviet Union. It is essential to modernize these strategic forces to maintain this capability as weapons age and Soviet capability improves. But current efforts are excessively redundant. The Air Force is working on five different ways to penetrate Soviet air defenses. It is upgrading the B-52 bomber force; it has produced the ALCM-B (an air-launched cruise missile) and is about to produce the ACM (another and more advanced air-launched cruise missile); it is proceeding with a rapid acquisition of one hundred or more B-1B bombers; and it is continuing a large-scale program for the early production of a "stealth" bomber that Soviet radars would find difficult to detect. At the same time that all these systems are rapidly being developed, the Air Force and the Navy are proceeding with two costly ballistic missiles—the land-based MX (or Peacekeeper) and the submarine-based Trident D-5—each designed to have a high probability of destroying a Soviet missile silo with a single warhead. Perhaps the only significant difference between the two missiles is that the D-5 will be much more survivable than the MX. Without in any way damaging the ability of the United States to penetrate Soviet air defenses or to destroy hardened targets with ballistic missiles, the B-1B bomber and the MX missile could be canceled. The saving in fiscal year 1985 alone would amount to more than $13 billion in budget authority (see table 4-4).

General-Purpose Forces

Less spectacular but still substantial savings can be achieved by reducing the production of both short-range tactical nuclear weapons and conventional weaponry for general-purpose forces. There is very little point in deploying the nuclear Tomahawk cruise missile (TLAM-N) on board attack submarines when the decision to place land-based Pershing II ballistic missiles and ground-launched cruise missiles (GLCMs) in Western Europe is already being implemented. Nor does it make much sense to allow the Army to modernize its antiaircraft defenses by upgrading the existing Vulcan, Chaparral, and Hawk guns and missiles and simultaneously buying new and unproved weapons (particularly the Sergeant York gun and the Patriot missile) for the same purposes, especially since the Patriot's capabilities compete with those of the Air Force's F-16 fighter. Cutting the Tomahawk program by half and canceling Sergeant York and Patriot would save more than $2.2 billion in fiscal year 1985 budget authority (see table 4-4).

The proliferation of fighter and attack aircraft is even greater. The Army is producing an expensive attack helicopter, the AH-64, which duplicates the function of an Air Force close-air-support aircraft, the A-10. The Air Force is preparing to acquire an attack version of the F-15 fighter at the same time that it buys the F-16 fighter already designed for attack missions. The Navy simultaneously continues production of the F-18 fighter and its A-18 attack version, the A6-E attack aircraft, the AV-8B attack aircraft for the Marines, and the F-14 fighter with its expensive Phoenix missile. By concentrating on the F-16 for the Air Force and the F-18 and A-18 for the Navy and Marines, $5.4 billion in budget authority could be saved in fiscal year 1985 (see table 4-4). Maintenance and logistics for the four air forces would be greatly simplified in the process.

Altogether, about $10 billion in procurement, development, military construction, and spare parts can be saved in fiscal year 1985 by eliminating this kind of duplication in the general-purpose forces—in addition to the $13 billion saved by eliminating the MX and the B-1B.

Slowing the Pace of Investment

In determining investment strategy, it is useful to view the defense establishment as possessing a collection of capital goods that have to be operated and maintained and replaced from time to time. The frequency of the replacement in peacetime will depend on the strength of prospective enemies, the pace of technological change, and the rate at which the particular capital good deteriorates. As with automobiles, it is possible to replace the equipment to keep up with or stay ahead of the Joneses, run the equipment into the ground, or stretch the life of the system through regular maintenance and repair. Even when this last strategy is adopted, however, it eventually becomes more efficient to buy a new item than to keep repairing the old one. For example, tracked vehicles are expected to have useful service lives of fifteen years, surface ships thirty years, submarines twenty-five years, and missiles and aircraft twenty years, even when they have undergone several major overhauls during their lives. On these assumptions the average turnover time for defense capital goods would be about twenty years—that is, if technology offered no prospect of a great leap forward and potential enemies were following essentially the same replacement strategy.

If the only factor affecting the replacement value of the capital stock were inflation, calculating investment costs would be a simple matter. However, precisely because of technological change and competition from potential enemies, the replacement value of an item from one generation to the next can go up in real terms by a factor of two or more, depending on the speed of the turnover and the discipline exercised in the design of the replacement. Thus a contemporary version of the B-52 bomber, the last of which cost $12.5 million in 1962, probably could not be bought for less than $160 million in fiscal year 1985, allowing for technological improvements and inflation during the last twenty-three years. By contrast, B-1B bombers, which are scheduled to replace some of the B-52s, will probably cost at least $300 million each. Because of such changes, it is often assumed that, on the average, the replacement value of defense weapons should rise in real terms by about 5 percent a year—as should the budget for investment—and that the next generation of weapons will cost in real terms about 2.7 times more than the generation it is replacing.

Because of such considerations, an investment strategy should be flexible with respect to the length of time between replacements, the sequencing of those replacements, and the real growth in costs to be allowed from one generation of equipment to the next. Nevertheless, barring an unexpected change in Soviet practices or dramatic technological developments, the United States would be prudent to adopt a long-term investment strategy that is substantially more orderly than the current costly rush to modernize. First, such a strategy would call for the replacement of the current inventory of capital equipment, on the average, only at the end of normal service life, although acquisition priorities would be established and particular systems such as tracked vehicles and aircraft would obviously be bought in large lots. Second, the annual investment budget would be allowed real increases of no more than 5 percent a year (and preferably less) to reflect the need to overhaul and upgrade the existing inventory and to replace it gradually with new equipment. Third, because these replacements would occur on the average every twenty years and their costs would be well known in advance, research, development, testing, and evaluation of new systems would be a more measured and orderly process than it now is, without the pressure to rush new and untried weapons into the inventory.

In the short run, modest reductions of $3.1 billion in fiscal year 1985 budget authority can be achieved simply by slowing the pace at which a number of weapons are being acquired (see table 4-5). Such reductions would ensure more orderly replacement policies in the future and perhaps help ease inflation. These effects, especially if combined with a more rigorous standardization of equipment than is now practiced, would more than offset any rise in unit prices caused by lower (but still large) production runs.

Eliminating Programs Based on Questionable Objectives

Even greater savings can be achieved by abandoning several of the more questionable objectives being pursued (see table 4-6). There is no need to engage in a rapid modernization of North American defenses against bombers when the main threat to U.S. targets comes from Soviet ballistic missiles. And while a leakproof defense against ballistic missiles may be desirable, no such defense is within reach. At most, research on both land-based and space-based means of engaging enemy

Table 4-5. *Savings from Slowing the Pace of Replacing and Upgrading Weapons, Fiscal Year 1985*
Billions of dollars of budget authority

Program	Action	Savings
M-1 Abrams tank	Reduce from 720 to 600	0.3
M-2 Bradley fighting vehicle	Reduce from 710 to 600	0.2
TOW-2 antitank guided missile	Reduce from 21,822 to 13,000	0.1
Light armored vehicle (LAV)	Reduce from 292 to 120	0.2
Multiple-launch rocket system (MLRS)	Reduce from 50,472 to 25,236	0.3
Hellfire antiarmor missile	Reduce from 6,026 to 4,000	0.1
Ground mobile forces satellite communications	Reduce from 200 to 130	0.1
High-mobility multi-purpose wheeled vehicle (HMMWV)	Reduce from 14,578 to 7,289	0.2
Heavy expanded-mobility tactical truck (HEMTT)	Reduce from 1,181 to 591	0.1
F-16 fighter-attack aircraft	Reduce from 150 to 120	0.8
F/A-18 fighter and attack aircraft	Reduce from 84 to 72	0.4
EA-6B electronic warfare aircraft	Reduce from 6 to 3	0.2
P-3C antisubmarine warfare patrol aircraft	Reduce from 9 to 6	0.2
Total savings	. . .	3.1

Sources: *Department of Defense Annual Report, Fiscal Year 1985*, pp. 113–202; and author's estimates. Numbers are rounded.

missiles should be conducted on an exploratory basis. At least $1.7 billion can be saved in fiscal year 1985 if the United States is realistic about what is feasible in the realm of defense against nuclear attacks and cancels modernization of continental air defense and procurement of space defense systems, for instance.

Savings of another $1 billion can be achieved in fiscal year 1985 by acknowledging that land-based ballistic missiles have outlived their usefulness in the United States and that neither the United States nor the Soviet Union understands how to achieve any meaningful objective by means of a nuclear war,

Table 4-6. *Savings from Eliminating or Reducing Programs Based on Questionable Objectives, Fiscal Year 1985*
Billions of dollars of budget authority

Program	Action	Savings
Strategic programs		
Small ICBM and mobile launcher	Cancel	0.5
Follow-on ICBM basing technology	Cancel	0.3
Strategic command centers	Cancel systems for protracted war	0.3
Continental air defense modernization	Cancel	0.4
Space defense systems	Cancel procurement	0.1
Strategic defense initiative	Reduce by 75 percent	1.3
Navy capabilities		
Aircraft carrier service life extension	Cancel	0.8
Battleship reactivation	Cancel	0.5
CG-47 Aegis air defense cruiser	Cancel 3 ships	3.2
DDG-51 Aegis air defense destroyer	Cancel	1.3
SSN-688 nuclear attack submarine	Reduce from 4 to 2	1.5
LHD-1 amphibious assault ship	Cancel	*
LSD-41 landing ship dock	Cancel	0.5
TAO fleet oiler	Reduce from 3 to 2	0.2
E-2C early warning aircraft	Reduce from 6 to 3	0.2
Airlift capacity		
C-5B airlift aircraft	Cancel	2.2
KC-10 advanced cargo-tanker aircraft	Reduce from 8 to 4	0.4
C-17 airlift aircraft	Cancel	0.1
Personnel requirements		
Military personnel	Reduce by 144,000	2.9
Civilian personnel	Reduce by 43,000	0.9
Family housing	Reduce to fiscal 1983 level	0.2
Military construction	Reduce to fiscal 1983 level	1.0
Total savings	. . .	18.7

Sources: *Department of Defense Annual Report, Fiscal Year 1985*, pp. 113–202; and author's estimates. Numbers are rounded.
* Less than $50 million.

protracted or otherwise. Small, mobile ICBMs, each armed
with a single warhead, may sound attractive as an alternative
to the MX, but the areas in which the United States can operate
mobile missiles are so confined that both areas and missiles
would be vulnerable to relatively simple and cheap attacks by
an enemy. And while survivable command-control-communi-
cations systems (C^3) are essential to nuclear retaliation, the case
for trying to ensure long endurance for these systems remains
weak because the concept of protracted nuclear war is so
unrealistic.

Several objectives for the general-purpose forces are equally
questionable. The idea that the Navy should take the offensive
with carrier battle groups and amphibious forces against naval
ports in the Soviet Union, and that it should expand capabilities
for such a purpose, is a prescription for high costs—about $8
billion in fiscal year 1985—and potential disaster. Vulnerable
sea-based forces would have to attack Soviet land-based forces
of great strength.

This is not to say that carrier battle groups and amphibious
forces no longer have a role in U.S. military planning. Both
amphibious assault ships with Marines on board and carrier
battle groups have been justified on the grounds that they
contribute to peacetime stability and deterrence by their presence in the western Pacific and the Mediterranean. More to
the point, each can generate tactical air and ground power and
establish a foothold on land in areas where nearby facilities for
land-based forces do not exist or where they are denied to the
United States. Thus the real issue in determining the size of
these specialized and costly forces is whether enough contingencies exist to justify maintaining them and, if so, for how
many such contingencies the Navy should be prepared.

It seems reasonable to plan that amphibious forces and
carrier battle groups might be needed in the Persian Gulf, the
Atlantic or Mediterranean, and the Far East. Intervention in
any of these areas could require, at least for initial operations,
as many as three carrier battle groups and enough amphibious
assault ships for a Marine brigade. Allowing for a wartime
deployment of nine battle groups and assuming that three
more would be in overhaul or refresher training at any one

time, the Navy would need twelve carrier battle groups and amphibious ships for a little more than a Marine division. Serious justification for three more carriers, four battleships, and more amphibious ships remains to be provided.

Another questionable goal is to expand airlift capacity. While it is essential to U.S. strategy that the armed forces have the ability to move large and heavy tactical air and ground forces to overseas areas of vital interest, it is highly questionable that more than doubling the airlift capacity of the Air Force to 66 million ton-miles a day is worth the $2.7 billion allotted in the fiscal year 1985 budget. While 66 million ton-miles sounds like a great deal of tonnage, in thirty days perhaps only five heavy divisions could be moved to Europe with the proposed force, compared with the two heavy divisions that could be deployed with existing aircraft. To the extent that additional long-range mobility is needed, fast ships are much cheaper per ton-mile and can deliver substantially more tonnage in thirty days for the same cost.

These questionable nuclear and nonnuclear objectives not only provide the excuse for additional weapons and equipment, but also justify adding military and civilian personnel, increasing the need for military family housing and expanding the budget for military construction. By discarding such objectives it becomes possible to reduce personnel and construction requirements to earlier levels at a saving in fiscal year 1985 budget authority of about $5 billion (see table 4-6). The reductions in personnel can be readily achieved by normal attrition.

All told, savings from eliminating unnecessary duplication, slowing the excessive pace of weapons replacement, and eliminating or reducing programs based on questionable objectives would amount to more than $45 billion in fiscal year 1985 budget authority. According to the estimates of the Congressional Budget Office, another $7.3 billion in budget authority could be saved by implementing the more specific recommendations of the President's Private Sector Survey on Cost Control (the Grace Commission).[2] These savings have not

2. *Analysis of the Grace Commission's Major Proposals for Cost Control,* Joint Study by the Congressional Budget Office and the General Accounting Office (GPO, February 1984), p. 27.

Table 4-7. *Comparison of Alternative Defense Budgets,*
by Appropriation Account, Fiscal Year 1985
Billions of dollars

Appropriation account	Reagan	Efficient Reagan	High threat	Low threat
Military personnel	52.9	50.0	50.8	46.5
Retired military pay	17.6	17.6	17.6	17.6
Operation and maintenance	81.4	80.5	81.9	74.9
Procurement	107.6	73.2	77.1	75.1
Research, development, test, and evaluation	34.0	28.3	28.3	27.6
Military construction	7.2	6.0	6.0	5.9
Family housing and homeowners' assistance	3.2	3.0	3.0	2.7
Revolving and management funds	1.8	1.8	1.8	1.8
Total obligational authority	305.7	260.4	266.5	252.1
Financial adjustments	−0.7	−0.7	−0.7	−0.7
Budget authority	305.0	259.7	265.8	251.4

Sources: *Budget of the United States Government, Fiscal Year 1985*, p. 5-10; and author's estimates.

been included here. However, they could be considered as an offset to any shortfall in the savings estimated to result from canceling major weapons programs.

How these savings would affect the defense budget for fiscal year 1985 (as submitted in February 1984) is shown in table 4-7 as the "efficient Reagan defense budget." This budget would require budget authority of $260 billion in fiscal year 1985. The largest change would occur in the procurement account—a reduction of $34.4 billion (or 32 percent). Research, development, testing, and evaluation would decline by 17 percent, and military construction would fall by an equal percentage. All other appropriation accounts would remain at the levels originally proposed by the administration except insofar as they reflect the reduction of military personnel from 2,194,000 to 2,050,000 and civilian personnel from 993,000 to 950,000. Over the five-year period, outlays under the efficient Reagan budget would be about $175 billion less than under the administration's original plan (see table 4-8).[3]

3. These savings use as a baseline the administration's own projections of what it will spend over the next five years. In calculating the savings expected from this defense program in chapter 1, we instead use the CBO baseline defense spending projections because the overall deficit is based on CBO expenditure and revenue projections. The savings projected here are slightly larger than those shown in table 1-1 because the administration projects a higher baseline than does the CBO.

Table 4-8. *Savings from Reagan Budget Outlays for Alternative Budget Possibilities, Fiscal Years 1985–89*
Billions of dollars

Budget	1985	1986	1987	1988	1989	Five-year total
High threat	7.5	21.3	35.4	40.9	38.5	143.6
Efficient Reagan	10.9	26.7	42.1	48.3	46.3	174.3
Low threat	18.2	38.3	59.0	72.4	78.8	266.7

Source: William W. Kaufmann, *The 1985 Defense Budget* (Brookings Institution, forthcoming), table 18.

The Reagan defense plan can be looked at as an expensive way to achieve deterrence in a world in which several moderate threats but no major ones are expected. We have also costed a "high-threat" alternative designed to cope with a more dangerous environment in which multiple crises, two of them large-scale threats, could arise simultaneously. The high-threat budget calls for increased expenditure for equipment and training to increase the readiness of National Guard and reserve ground forces and airwings. With savings from eliminating duplication and questionable objectives, the high-threat budget would still cost about $144 billion less in 1985–89 than the budget the administration has proposed (see table 4-8). A "low-threat" budget appropriate to a less threatening international environment would entail even larger savings than the efficient Reagan budget. Calling for lower levels of combat readiness and slower growth in procurement, the low-threat alternative would save $267 billion in outlays in 1985–89 (see table 4-8).

Summary

Strengthening U.S. military forces through increases in defense spending has been a primary commitment of the Reagan administration. Most of this increased spending has gone to upgrade the equipment of the armed services. Despite the growth in spending, however, the United States will achieve no concomitant increase in the capabilities of its nuclear and conventional forces. Nor is it clear that such an increase is needed: the Reagan administration's basic defense strategy is not a major departure from that established in the mid-1970s, the armed forces have experienced considerable renovation already, and the Soviet defense buildup in the last ten years has been moderate. The rapid budget increases, however, are creating an enormous backlog in budget authority, much of it committed and uncontrollable, and are inviting block obsolescence of equipment in the future. Both these consequences make attempts to control defense spending much more difficult.

The United States could achieve significant reductions in costs without weakening the nation's defense or altering basic strategy. Three actions would account for most of the potential savings: eliminating the duplication of programs within and among the services, moderating the pace of modernization, and abandoning programs based on questionable assumptions or unrealistic objectives. These actions could result in an efficient budget that would achieve the administration's goals at a saving of nearly $175 billion during fiscal years 1985–89.

5

Reforming the Tax System

REDUCING the federal deficit by the amounts proposed in this book will require raising taxes. The current federal tax system will simply not generate enough revenue to pay for even the reduced expenditure program set forth in the previous chapters. Furthermore, the current tax system is riddled with special provisions that affect taxpayers in similar circumstances very differently and needlessly reduce economic efficiency. Simply raising tax rates would compound these inequities and ineffi- ciencies. We believe the system needs thorough reform.

Various approaches to reform are possible. Some would broaden the base of the individual income tax by ending most exclusions and deductions (often known as "loopholes") so that additional revenue can be obtained without raising tax rates. Others argue for shifting in part from a tax on income to one on consumption by enacting a value-added tax or national sales tax. Our proposal combines both ideas: broad- ening the base and taxing spending rather than income. We would replace both the individual income tax and the estate and gift tax with an individual cash flow tax. This would mean restructuring the current individual tax so that the tax base would become income from all sources minus net saving, and then taxing this base at progressive rates. We would also

Henry J. Aaron and Harvey Galper undertook primary responsibility for drafting this chapter.

convert the corporation income tax into a cash flow tax under which corporations would be taxed on their receipts minus current expenses, including investment. This new tax system would not be free of problems—no perfect tax exists—but we believe it would be fairer, simpler, and more favorable to economic growth than the present system.

Such a major change in tax laws could not be put in place quickly enough to produce the added revenue needed to bring down the deficit in the next two or three years. We therefore propose an interim tax program combining some immediate broadening of the tax base with a temporary income tax surcharge.

This chapter briefly reviews the inadequacies of the present tax structure.[1] It then describes the new system we are proposing and compares the proposed tax system with the present one. It ends with a discussion of alternative approaches to tax reform. It does not, however, propose any shifts in tax burdens among economic classes. Such changes may be desirable, but any attempt to achieve them now would vastly complicate the already-formidable task of designing politically acceptable tax reform. Revenues must be increased and the tax structure must be reformed as the first order of business. Then the nation should debate whether the present distribution of tax burdens should be changed.

Indictment of the Current Tax System

Federal revenue for purposes other than social security and medicare comes primarily from taxes on personal and corporation incomes. Ideally, income taxes should be simple, straightforward levies that apportion the burden of paying for government according to each taxpayer's ability to pay. They should be fair in the sense that taxpayers in the same circumstances should pay the same tax. And they should not interfere with economic efficiency by biasing economic choices. At present,

---

1. This chapter deals exclusively with problems under the personal and corporation income taxes. It does not examine the payroll tax, which is linked to social security cash and medical benefits and to unemployment insurance. Nor does it consider the structure of excise taxes or possible additional taxes on energy.

however, a prosecuting attorney would have no difficulty persuading an impartial jury to convict the federal income tax system on several counts: it diverts resources away from their most productive uses, it is complex, and it is unfair.

First, the tax system distorts investment. Largely because of unrealistic depreciation deductions, the investment tax credit, and inflation-related distortions, effective tax rates on investment differ enormously from one type of investment to another. As a result, investment is diverted from its most productive uses—those with the highest rates of return before tax—into less productive uses. This harms overall growth.

Second, the tax system distorts compensation. Because employer-provided fringe benefits such as health and life insurance are not taxed to employees like other income, the system encourages compensation in the form of these benefits even when the cost is greater than the amount that employees would be willing to pay in cash for them. This is wasteful.

Third, the tax system distorts saving. If income is saved in certain forms, such as specific kinds of pension and retirement accounts, the income and interest earnings on it are taxed only when withdrawn from these accounts. Other kinds of saving are not so favorably treated. As a result, people who are saving the same amount face different tax rates. It is even possible for people to avoid tax by moving money from one account to another without actually increasing saving.

Fourth, the tax system needlessly penalizes work. Because of the numerous exclusions, deductions, and credits that give rise to the preceding inefficiencies, the tax base is greatly constricted. That means that the tax rate on wages and salaries, most of which are taxable, must be much higher than it would be if the base were larger. This makes work less rewarding.

Fifth, the tax system is appallingly complex. Much of the complexity arises from a morass of special provisions that makes the tax form all but incomprehensible. One whole industry has arisen to sell advice on how to shelter income legally, and another to help people fill c it their returns. In the business world, success increasingly rests on the ability to minimize taxes, rather than on knowledge of how to innovate, cut costs, or market effectively.

Finally, and partly as a result of all of the above, the tax system is just plain unfair. Many people suspect that if the tax system is too complex for them to understand, it must be cheating them. And they are right, because those who can hire tax experts to plan their affairs do avoid taxes that ordinary citizens pay.

Each of the many special credits, deductions, and exclusions that complicate the tax code has some appeal when viewed in isolation. Taken together, however, they partially offset each other and result in a tax system that produces unrecognized and unintended effects, bewilders taxpayers, and undermines the faith of ordinary citizens in the laws to which they are subject. In summary, the tax system produces too little revenue and too many inequities and inefficiencies.

The Short-Run Program

The urgent need is to increase revenues by about $108 billion in fiscal year 1989, the amount shown in table 1-1. One way to raise revenues quickly would be to postpone all attempts to reform the tax system and simply enact a surcharge: taxpayers would compute their income tax liability and then add a fixed percentage. A better approach would be to broaden the base of personal and corporation income taxes, provided that actions taken now do not foreclose desirable long-run reforms. Such a strategy could contribute to improvements in fairness, efficiency, and administration at the same time it would help to close the deficit. The long-run agenda set forth below calls for a comprehensive tax base that would include all receipts minus all net saving. Short-run base broadening reforms are consistent with this program if they expand the definition of taxable receipts and disallow deductions unrelated to saving. Table 5-1 presents a selected list of such measures. If all these proposals were enacted, they would raise $30 billion in 1985, increasing to $95 billion in 1989.

Such a program of short-run base broadening could go a long way toward meeting the revenue goals set forth in this book, but it is highly unlikely that a consensus on these matters can be achieved very quickly. We therefore urge enactment of

Table 5-1. *Revenue Gains from Selected Proposals to Broaden the Tax Base, Fiscal Years 1985–89*
Billions of dollars

Proposal	1985	1986	1987	1988	1989
Eliminate tax-exempt bonds for private purposes	0.4	1.5	2.9	4.1	5.4
Repeal deduction for nonmortgage interest in excess of investment income	1.8	9.6	10.6	11.6	12.7
Repeal deduction for state sales taxes	0.8	5.6	6.3	7.2	8.1
Repeal charitable deduction for nonitemizers	0.2	1.7	2.8	0	0
Repeal 15 percent net interest exclusion	1.0	2.9	3.1	3.4	3.6
Tax employees on employer contributions to health plans[a]	3.9	6.5	8.0	9.7	12.1
Tax workers' compensation income replacement benefits	1.6	2.4	2.7	2.9	3.2
Tax unemployment benefits fully	*	1.4	1.4	1.3	1.2
Tax veterans' compensation benefits	1.5	2.3	2.3	2.4	2.5
Tax 50 percent of social security and railroad retirement benefits	2.2	6.7	6.8	6.8	6.8
Tax nonstatutory fringe benefits	0.5	0.7	0.8	0.9	1.0
Tax employees on employer-provided group life insurance	1.8	2.7	3.0	3.3	3.6
Cut business deductions for entertainment by 50 percent	0.6	1.2	1.4	1.5	1.6
Repeal preferences for DISC (export-oriented) corporations	0.9	2.0	2.5	2.7	2.9
Restrict tax-exempt leasing	1.7	2.7	4.0	5.4	7.0
Curtail tax shelter, accounting, and corporate tax abuse[a]	3.2	4.3	4.7	5.7	6.6
Maintain foreign earned-income exclusion at 1983 level	*	0.1	0.1	0.1	0.1
Eliminate employer stock ownership tax credit	1.3	2.2	2.3	1.0	*
Maintain estate and gift tax credit and rates at 1984 level	0	0.9	1.7	2.5	3.1
Eliminate capital gains treatment of timber	0.3	0.7	0.8	0.8	0.8
Repeal deduction for excess bad-debt reserves	0.6	0.9	1.0	1.0	1.1
Repeal reduced rates on first $100,000 of corporate income	4.8	8.7	9.4	9.8	10.1
Repeal percentage depletion allowance	0.6	1.1	1.2	1.3	1.3
Total	29.7	68.8	79.8	85.4	94.8

Sources: Congressional Budget Office, *Reducing the Deficit: Spending and Revenue Options* (CBO, February 1983), p. 296; CBO, *Reducing the Deficit: Spending and Revenue Options* (CBO, February 1984), pp. 201–04, 209, 213, 215, 216, 220, 224, 227, 233, 240; CBO, *An Analysis of the President's Budgetary Proposals for Fiscal Year 1985* (CBO, February 1984), p. 26; CBO, *Tax Expenditures: Current Issues and Five-Year Budget Projections for Fiscal Years 1984–1988* (CBO, October 1983), pp. 52, 56; *Tax Reform Act of 1984*, H. Rept. 98-432, pt. 2, 98 Cong. 2 sess. (Government Printing Office, 1984), pp. 1123, 1124; and authors' estimates.
* Less than $50 million.
a. As proposed in the administration's 1985 budget.

a surtax that when added to the revenues provided by short-run base-broadening reforms would assure that the revenue goals presented in table 1-1 are met. If half the short-run base-broadening reforms were enacted, they would meet the revenue goals for 1985 with only a 2 percent surcharge. If none were enacted, a surcharge of 6 percent would be necessary to meet these goals. By 1989, however, the tax increase required to meet these targets is so large—$108 billion—that to reach them would require either a surcharge of 19 percent or enactment of half the base-broadening measures plus a 10.5 percent surcharge on personal and corporation incomes.

Any surcharge would raise rates levied on a still-distorted tax base and aggravate the distortion between fully taxed activities and partially taxed or exempt activities. Only the overriding need for reducing the deficit would justify these added distortions, even on a temporary basis. A surcharge would stand out from the fundamental tax structure, under-scoring its temporary nature, and would emphasize that work on long-run base broadening must begin immediately. Furthermore, although the short-run base-broadening measures shown in table 5-1 are a source of substantial structural improvement, they do not correct most of the deficiencies of the current tax system noted above. These reforms raise most of the political problems presented by fundamental tax reform, but even their complete enactment would leave serious inequities and inefficiencies in the tax code.

The Long-Run Program

The goals of any tax system should be to collect revenues fairly, with minimal disturbance to economic efficiency and growth, according to rules that taxpayers can comply with and administrators can enforce. In practice, of course, no system can completely realize all of these partially conflicting goals. But in our view the U.S. tax system is now so cluttered and inconsistent that it fails on all counts. Several approaches to reform exist—any one of which could provide a tax system at once fairer, less inefficient, and simpler than the one now in effect.

At present, the United States obtains some 45 percent of its revenues from what is called an individual "income" tax, but which on examination turns out to be something quite different. For one thing, a large share of income is not subject to tax. Most fringe benefits provided by employers, for example, are not taxed as part of employees' compensation. Most transfer payments remain untaxed, despite the recent inclusion of some unemployment insurance and social security benefits in taxable income. Much capital income is never taxed. Income that is saved in certain forms and the interest income on that saving can be deferred. The tax treatment of such sheltered accounts as Keogh plans, individual retirement accounts, and qualified pension plans has moved the so-called income tax substantially toward being a tax on consumption (or income minus saving).

In fact, the coexistence of income and consumption tax rules in the present tax structure poses a fundamental choice in charting a program of basic tax reform. Should the major tax on individuals be based on the principle that all income should be taxed? Or should it be based on the principle that all expenditures should be taxed, but that saving or investment should be exempt until consumed?

The choice between a comprehensive tax on income or one on expenditures should not hinge on the mistaken belief that the present system closely resembles one or the other or that it would be significantly easier to attain one rather than the other. The present tax system is far removed from both. The attainment of either will involve enormous changes, but they cannot be avoided if the goal is to undo the effects of inconsistent provisions accumulated over the past seventy years.

The proposal advanced here is based on the premise that a greater degree of fairness, economic efficiency, and administrative simplicity can be achieved by establishing a consistent expenditure or cash flow tax than by trying to establish a consistent income tax. We recognize that the real world is too complex and varied to permit genuine simplicity in taxation and that all practical taxes involve some distortions and unfairness. But we believe this proposal would be a substantial improvement over the present system.

The Tax on Individuals. We propose that people be taxed at the household level (as at present), but on their cash flow, not their income.[2] Each taxpaying unit would be taxed on all cash receipts, minus net saving. Both receipts and savings would be comprehensively defined. Receipts would include all wages and salaries, rent, interest, profits, dividends, transfer payments, gifts received, and inheritances. Savings would include all net payments into certain "qualified accounts," including all financial assets (stocks, bonds, and other securities), all accounts in banks and other depository institutions, the cash value of life insurance, and real estate (except owner-occupied housing, for reasons set forth below).

Just as additions to saving would be deducted from income, such dissaving as the sale of stock or withdrawal from a bank account would be added to the tax base. Similarly, the proceeds from loans would be included in the tax base, and loan repayments, including both principal and interest, would be deducted from receipts in calculating the tax base.

Inheritances would be counted as a receipt, but if they were not consumed, they would be exactly offset by an increase in savings. Gifts and bequests would be treated as spending in the year in which they were made, subject to an averaging provision if the amounts transferred were large relative to annual cash flow.

It would be desirable to award each person a lifetime

2. The material in this book draws heavily on recent writings on the consumption tax. Although specific attributions have not always been made throughout the chapter, the interested reader may wish to consult the following sources: William D. Andrews, "A Consumption-Type or Cash Flow Personal Income Tax," *Harvard Law Review*, vol. 87 (April 1974), pp. 1113–88; Anthony B. Atkinson and Joseph E. Stiglitz, *Lectures on Public Economics* (McGraw-Hill, 1980), especially chap. 3; David F. Bradford, "The Economics of Tax Policy Toward Savings," in George M. von Furstenberg, ed., *The Government and Capital Formation* (Ballinger, 1980), pp. 11–71; David F. Bradford, "Issues in the Design of Savings and Investment Incentives," in Charles R. Hulten, ed., *Depreciation, Inflation, and the Taxation of Income from Capital* (Washington, D.C.: Urban Institute, 1981), pp. 13–47; Robert E. Hall and Alvin Rabushka, *Low Tax, Simple Tax, Flat Tax* (McGraw-Hill, 1983); Sven-Olof Lodin, *Progressive Expenditure Tax—An Alternative?* a report of the 1972 Government Commission on Taxation (Stockholm: LiberFörlag, 1978); *The Structure and Reform of Direct Taxation*, report of a committee chaired by J. E. Meade for the Institute for Fiscal Studies (London: George Allen and Unwin, 1978); Peter Mieszkowski, "The Advisability and Feasibility of an Expenditure Tax System," in Henry J. Aaron and Michael J. Boskin, eds., *The Economics of Taxation* (Brookings Institution, 1980), pp. 179–201; Joseph A. Pechman, ed., *What Should be Taxed: Income or Expenditure?* (Brookings Institution, 1980); and U.S. Treasury Department, *Blueprints for Basic Tax Reform* (Government Printing Office, 1977).

Table 5-2. *Tax-Free Levels of Income or Consumption*
under Current Tax Law and under Proposed Cash Flow Tax
Dollars

Household size and composition	Current tax (income)	Proposed tax (cash flow)
Single	3,300	5,000
Couple, no children	5,400	8,250
Couple, one child	6,400	9,750
Couple, two children	7,400	11,250

exemption for making a certain amount of gifts or bequests in order to permit tax-free transfers, such as those between parents and children, at time of need. A lifetime exemption of $100,000 per person ($200,000 per couple) would permit most families to exclude all gifts and bequests from tax. Under the cash flow tax, taxation of gifts and bequests over the exemption amount would be a substitute for current taxation under the federal estate and gift tax, which could then be repealed.[3]

The inclusion of both inheritances and bequests in the cash flow tax base is essential to fulfill the principle of fairness in taxation, explained in more detail below. If they are included, the cash flow tax base would correctly measure resources available to each person over his or her lifetime.

Personal exemptions would be allowed as under the present personal income tax, although the amount should be modified. We propose as a minimum standard that no tax be imposed on people whose consumption is less than current poverty thresholds. Based on estimates for 1984, tax-free levels of consumption would be set at $5,000 for a single person, $8,250 for couples, and $1,500 for each additional dependent (see table 5-2). In addition, some account should be taken of the fact that one-earner families are better off than two-earner families with the same income. Two-earner families lose in-home services provided by the nonearning spouse in a one-earner household and may incur money costs for child care and other household

3. To justify a wealth transfer tax in addition to the inclusion of bequests in the cash flow tax, one would have to go beyond the notion that equals are defined in terms of income flows over their lifetimes and argue that large accumulations of wealth are undesirable per se and should be a separate object of taxation.

services. Accordingly, we recommend the continued deduction of 10 percent of the earnings of the spouse with lesser earnings, up to some maximum level (the limit under current law is $30,000 per year).[4] Similarly, a credit for low earners, like the earned-income tax credit now allowed certain workers with low earnings, might be provided.

Tax rates would be progressive under the cash flow tax. Because the base for the cash flow tax is broader than that for the current personal income tax, the same revenues could be raised with lower rates. For joint returns, existing revenues could be matched with a 5 percent tax on the first $10,000 of taxable expenditures, 20 percent on the next $30,000 of taxable expenditures, and 32 percent on taxable expenditures over $40,000 per year. For single persons, the same rates would apply to taxable expenditure brackets of 0 to $5,000, $5,000 to $40,000, and over $40,000. To raise the additional $108 billion called for in table 1-1, these rates would have to become 6 percent, 24 percent, and 38 percent. These rates would apply only to expenditures above tax-free ranges, defined by the enlarged personal exemptions and increased zero-bracket amounts. These rates would approximately reproduce the distribution of tax burdens under the current personal income tax, except for reductions in taxes among low-income taxpayers, who would benefit from the increased tax-free ranges.[5] For example, a four-person family would pay no tax on up to $11,250 of expenditures per year; in contrast, that same family is taxable under current law on income over $7,400 per year.

Because bequests would be included in the cash flow tax base (subject to averaging), burdens on taxpayers would be reduced throughout their working years and increased substantially at death. The main reason why taxation at death would be increased is that the cash flow tax on bequests would be designed to be harder to avoid than the present estate tax.[6]

4. This deduction would have the effect of increasing tax-free levels of consumption for two-earner families.

5. The ratio of the proposed cash flow tax to household expenditure would be the same as the ratio of the current income tax to household expenditure. Because consumption expenditures are much less variable over one's lifetime than income, we use expenditure (including bequests), rather than income, to classify households.

6. The calculation of the value of wealth transfers included in the tax base was based on a methodology developed by Daphne Greenwood in "An Estimation of U.S.

If no changes were made in the income tax base, the revenue targets set forth in this book could be met by increasing current rates, which range from 11 percent to 50 percent, to 13 to 59 percent. In contrast, the cash flow tax could meet these targets with rates ranging from 6 percent to 38 percent.

Except for personal exemptions, a working-spouse deduction, and the special deductions for limited amounts of wealth transfers, any further deductions, credits, or exclusions would represent a step away from the principles of fairness and efficiency described below. We recognize that rigorous adherence to this principle would terminate some of the most important and popular advantages conferred on particular sources or uses of income by the present tax laws. For example, all transfer payments would be potentially taxable; wealth would be taxed in full when consumed or transferred to another person; home mortgage interest would no longer be deductible; and deductions for state and local taxes would be disallowed. The relative tax advantage that debt of state and local governments enjoys because interest on it is exempt from federal tax would also end, as all capital income would be included in the tax base in full unless it was saved.

The pressure would be strong to retain many of these concessions, and a few should probably be retained. But it is vital to recognize that these and other special provisions bear much of the responsibility for the complexity, unfairness, and inefficiency of the present system. Moreover, each attempt to exempt a source or use of income from the tax base means that the tax rates would have to be raised to generate the same amount of revenue from the lower base.

The Tax on Business. Recent tax legislation has lowered the effective rate of corporate taxation, albeit erratically, and reduced the corporate tax to a minor source of federal revenue (about 10 percent of the total in fiscal 1984).

Scrapping the corporate tax altogether and taxing the income

Family Wealth and its Distribution from Microdata, 1973," *Review of Income and Wealth,* vol. 29 (March 1983), pp. 23–44. For an excellent discussion of estate tax avoidance, see George Cooper, *A Voluntary Tax? New Perspectives on Sophisticated Estate Tax Avoidance* (Brookings Institution, 1979). Effective implementation of the cash flow tax would require a major reduction in the opportunities for avoiding tax on wealth transfers.

generated by corporations only when it is paid out to individuals is an idea that has some appeal. Unfortunately, scrapping the corporate tax would raise three serious problems. First, the increasing amount of U.S. business income flowing to foreigners would escape taxation. Second, individuals would use the corporate form to avoid taxation. Corporations would be able to finance tax-free consumption for employees and stockholders by purchasing a wide variety of consumption goods, such as automobiles, housing, life insurance, health care, or legal services—indeed, almost anything. Third, repeal of the corporate income tax would represent a windfall gain for corporate owners of depreciable capital. For these reasons, we believe the corporate tax must be retained. But it should be reformed to make it neutral with respect to different types of investments and to discourage its use to avoid the personal cash flow tax.

The corporate tax we propose would have two parts. The first would be a tax on the cash flow of corporations. The corporation tax base would include total receipts of the corporation from all sources other than the sale of stock, less all business expenses, including investment. Deductions for business expenditures on consumption items for the benefit of employees or owners would be denied.[7] The business tax base would include the proceeds from borrowing. Corporations would be entitled to deduct all debt service payments, but no deductions would be permitted for dividends or any other cash distribution to stockholders.[8] If firms borrowed to finance investment, no tax would result in the year the investment was made; the expenditure on the investment would just offset the proceeds from the loan. If earnings on the investment differed from the repayment of debt, corporate cash flow and tax liabilities would be affected.[9]

7. Deductions for consumption expenditures by noncorporate businesses would also be denied.

8. The exclusion of both the proceeds from sale of stock and of dividends has the effect of exempting returns equal to the government's borrowing rate from tax at the business level.

9. The same principles would be applied to cash flow of noncorporate businesses. In particular, new investments and debt transactions would be treated in the same way. Net cash flow, however, would be included immediately in the tax base of the owners, although there would be an offsetting deduction for saving if the funds remained in the business or were saved.

The second element of the tax on corporations would be a withholding tax on all distributions from corporations to foreign individuals and corporations. This tax would apply to dividends, interest, rents, royalties, proceeds from liquidation, or any other cash distribution.

The corporate cash flow tax would complement the individual cash flow tax and would have major advantages over the present corporation income tax. It would do away with the need to engage in complex accounting for depreciation, as investment would be treated as a deductible expense at the time it is made.[10] It would avoid other inflation-related distortions in the definition of business income. It would avoid the complexities of defining long-term capital gains and the avenues for tax avoidance that this favored source of income creates. The cash flow tax would continue to impose tax on the income from capital in existence when the new system was adopted. In addition, it would minimize use of corporations to avoid the individual spending tax. The withholding tax would fall on payments abroad that are generated in the United States. The rate of the corporate cash flow tax would equal the maximum rate on personal cash flow.[11]

These proposals would cause major changes in the U.S. tax system and would have far-reaching effects. But the tax system is so riddled with ad hoc and contradictory rules entrenched in past personal and business decisions that any effort to establish a consistent and fair system will have similarly wrenching effects. For this reason, care is needed in devising

10. Immediate deduction of the cost of investments would generate tax losses for new firms or for firms otherwise earning small profits. For deductibility to be as valuable on investments undertaken by such firms as it would be for profitable firms, a variety of steps could be undertaken. Firms could be allowed to carry tax losses forward to be applied against future cash flow. If this course is followed, the losses should be accumulated with interest to assure that their present value does not decline over time, a potentially serious problem when interest rates are high. In addition, firms could be allowed to offset any current negative cash flow against previous positive cash flow and receive rebates of previous taxes paid, similar to tax-loss carrybacks allowed under current law. In principle, past taxes should also be increased by the discount factor, but so long as interest is paid on loss carryforwards, this additional refinement is of limited significance.

11. If revenues from the corporate tax differed from those yielded by the current corporation income tax, individual and corporate cash flow rates would have to be adjusted accordingly.

adequate transition rules and in dealing with special circumstances. The treatment of housing, education, and international
capital and investment flows, for example, requires particular
attention. Although some of these issues are examined briefly
below, we make no attempt here to analyze them in technical
detail.

But these problems should not prevent action. The consequence of failure to act will be perpetuation of unfairness,
inefficiency, and complexity. The gains in these areas would
fully justify the inevitable problems associated with transition.
The United States must begin now to reform its tax system.

Guiding Principles

No attempt at tax reform will succeed in greatly reducing
distortions and inequities if it is based merely on pragmatic
political considerations. In designing the proposed cash flow
tax on both individuals and businesses, we were guided by
the standards of fairness, efficiency and growth, and ease of
administration.

Fairness

Some problems that create unfairness and complexity in the
present tax system would disappear when the tax system we
propose is fully implemented. For example, under the current
system the measurement of capital income is distorted in
periods of inflation because inflation erodes the value of
deductions for capital depreciation. Inflation also distorts the
measurement of capital gains and losses, because the cost of
investments is recovered in dollars with lower purchasing
power than those used to acquire the assets. These distortions
would not occur under the cash flow taxes. All outlays for
saving or investment would be fully deductible in the year in
which they occur. For tax purposes, there would be no capital-
recovery allowances to be eroded over subsequent years by
inflation.

Similarly, the cash flow tax would solve the problem of
accrued versus realized gains that plagues the income tax. In

principle, the income tax rests on the "accretion concept" that additions to wealth in each period constitute an appropriate measure of ability to pay. That means that capital gains should be taxed as they accrue, for that is when they add to ability to pay. For practical reasons, however, most capital income is taxed when realized, not when the gain actually accrues to the taxpayer. As a result, two people or businesses with identical economic incomes may pay quite different taxes.[12] The inability as a practical matter to tax capital gains as they accrue means that any tax on realized income will be inequitable.

The distinction between realized and accrued income would disappear under the individual cash flow tax. Appreciating stock would be treated the same as a savings account that increases in value as interest is earned over time. In both cases, tax would be generated only when the asset is liquidated to finance consumption or transfers to other people. The amount a person can spend or transfer would be unaffected by the timing of the sale of an asset. Unrealized gains would be simply irrelevant.

Another problem of the current income tax is that people with the same spending opportunities over a lifetime pay widely differing amounts of tax depending on how their income is distributed over the life cycle. Those who choose to save their income for consumption late in life or for gifts to others are taxed more heavily than those who are less provident. Limited averaging provisions now in force ameliorate the effects of some, but not all, short-term fluctuations in income, but they do nothing to ameliorate the distortions from life cycle variations in income.

Under an annual income tax it is impossible in practice to ensure that people with the same lifetime capacity to consume, discounted to present value, pay equal lifetime taxes. But this

---

12. Thus, if person A enjoys a capital gain or suffers a capital loss on an asset that he retains, his taxes are unaffected by that gain or loss. If person B experiences the same gain or loss and sells the asset, his tax is affected. If person C has two assets, one of which appreciates and one of which declines in value by the same amount, his total economic income from both assets is zero. But if he sells the asset that has declined in value and retains the appreciated asset, the tax collector observes a loss for the year and the individual is able to subtract this loss, in whole or in part, from other income, thus reducing his tax.

principle of fairness in taxation, which we find compelling, can be achieved under a cash flow tax that taxes all uses of lifetime income—consumption, bequests, and gifts to others. Under a cash flow tax, whether one consumes early in life, saves for later consumption, or bequeaths an estate to one's heirs, the present value of all tax liabilities incurred over one's lifetime is unaffected.[13]

Efficiency and Growth

The benefits of a free market economy rest on the presumption that private economic decisions in the absence of taxation would channel resources into their most profitable uses and into consumption that results in maximum personal satisfaction. Virtually all taxes affect some economic decision—how much to save or to work, what to consume, or which investment to make. An "efficient" tax system—one that does minimal damage to profitability and consumer satisfaction—should change economic decisions as little as possible from those made in the absence of taxation. Deviations from this standard can be tolerated if the market is not working properly or if efficiency is to be sacrificed to some other goal, such as altering the distribution of income or encouraging socially worthy activities. But few of the distortions of the present tax system can be justified on these grounds. Particularly worrisome departures from efficiency are: (1) widely varying effective tax rates on

13. Economists should recognize that the cash flow tax base is simply the familiar Haig-Simons definition of income extended from one year to the lifetime, and expressed in present value terms. The equity objective of an equal present value of lifetime taxes for taxpayers with equal lifetime incomes can be realized in a strict sense only if tax rates are proportional rather than progressive. However, the expanded width of tax brackets under the cash flow tax, together with opportunities for averaging, implies a high degree of success in realizing this objective. The cash flow tax might also be called an "endowment" tax, because the base is the capacity of each person to spend over his or her lifetime. It is *not* the same as a consumption tax, which falls only on consumption but excludes changes in net worth by exempting gifts and bequests from the tax base. See Richard A. Musgrave, "ET, OT, and SBT," *Journal of Public Economics*, vol. 6 (July–August 1976), pp. 3–16; and Musgrave, "The Nature of Horizontal Equity and the Principle of Broad-based Taxation: A Friendly Critique," in John G. Head, ed., *Taxation Issues of the 1980s* (Melbourne: Australian Tax Research Foundation, 1983), pp. 21–33. For measures of the effects on a cash flow tax of excluding bequests and gifts, see Paul L. Menchik and Martin David, "The Incidence of a Lifetime Consumption Tax," *National Tax Journal*, vol. 35 (June 1982), pp. 189–203.

Table 5-3. *Effective Marginal Tax Rates on Investment, by Asset, Industry, Source of Finance, and Owner, 1980*

Investment	Effective tax rate
Type of asset	
Machinery	17.6
Building	41.1
Inventories	47.0
Industry	
Manufacturing	52.7
Other industry	14.6
Commerce	38.2
Source of finance	
Debt	− 16.3
New share issues	91.2
Retained earnings	62.4
Owner of asset	
Households	57.5
Tax-exempt institutions	− 21.5
Insurance companies	23.4
All investments	37.2

Source: Mervyn A. King and Don Fullerton, *The Taxation of Income from Capital: A Comparative Study of the United States, the United Kingdom, Sweden, and West Germany* (University of Chicago Press, 1984), p. 244.

different classes of savings and investments, and (2) tax treatment of saving that distorts decisions about whether to save or consume.

Investment Distortions. As may be seen in table 5-3, effective rates of tax on different classes of investments vary from 91.2 percent to − 21.5 percent (the latter a subsidy rather than a tax), depending on type of investment, industry, source of finance, and type of ownership. Within these categories the variation is even wider, ranging from tax rates of 111 percent on buildings financed by new shares sold to households in either manufacturing or commerce, to − 105 percent on machinery used in the commercial sector financed by debt sold to tax-exempt institutions.[14]

These variations in effective tax rates arise from the interaction of several features of the tax system. Tax depreciation

14. Mervyn A. King and Don Fullerton, eds., *The Taxation of Income from Capital: A Comparative Study of the United States, the United Kingdom, Sweden, and West Germany* (University of Chicago Press, 1984), pp. 299–300. This variation in effective tax rates has been significantly increased by legislation enacted since 1980.

bears little relation to true economic depreciation. The investment tax credit is available only on certain assets. Some investment income is taxed only at the personal level, some at both the corporate and personal levels. Effective tax rates also differ because of the method of finance, because of variations in the taxation of different financial institutions, and because some investors are taxable while others are wholly or partially exempt. The failure of the tax system to adjust the measurement of capital income for inflation increases these distortions.

The way in which varying rates distort profitability can be seen in an illustration. Suppose that type A investments are taxed at 80 percent, type B investments are taxed at 40 percent, and type C investments are untaxed. If these investments are equally risky, people will invest where the after-tax rate of return is highest. If type C investments yield 6 percent before and after tax, type B investments will have to earn 10 percent before tax in order to attract funds, and type A investments will have to earn 30 percent. That means that a type A investment that yields 29 percent before tax will lose out to a type C investment that yields only 6 percent. Nearly four-fifths of the potential return on the marginal dollars of investment would be lost because of distortions induced by this tax system.

Distortion of Saving and Consumption. The form of household saving is also distorted by wide variations in the taxation of different assets. Payments into qualified pensions and individual retirement accounts and income earned on such assets are untaxed until withdrawn. Interest on municipal bonds is untaxed at any time. Gains in the value of assets are untaxed until realized and are never taxed if the holder dies before realizing them. Up to $125,000 of capital gain on owner-occupied housing is exempted from tax if the owner does not realize the gain until age fifty-five. In contrast, interest on corporate and federal debt and most dividends are taxed in full if received by households. While the treatment of asset income is highly varied, expenses incurred in earning this income, including interest, are generally deductible.[15]

These inconsistent rules produce a pattern of wealth holding

15. Eugene Steuerle, "Is Income from Capital Subject to Individual Income Taxation?" *Public Finance Quarterly*, vol. 10 (July 1982), pp. 283–303.

quite different from what would appear optimal in their absence. In the pursuit of tax advantages, individuals may sacrifice liquidity or vary the degree of risk that they are willing to assume. Furthermore, households may be able to obtain tax benefits merely by changing the form of their saving or by borrowing in order to save in a tax-preferred form. It is even possible for these provisions to make an investment profitable that would be unprofitable in the absence of taxes.[16]

In addition to distorting the form of saving, the income tax also discourages people from providing for future consumption needs. When a person earns a dollar, he must decide whether to consume it now or to save it for later consumption or bequest. If there were no taxes, this decision would be based on each person's present wants and best guess about future wants and on the rate of return on savings. The personal income tax distorts this decision, because the return to saving is taxed. As a result, the income tax increases the cost of future consumption or, in other words, reduces the reward to saving.

The effect can be large. Suppose a thirty-year-old person is considering whether to consume income currently or to save it for retirement consumption thirty-five years later. Assume that the annual rate of return on saving is 10 percent. In the absence of taxes, that person must give up $35 of current consumption for each $1,000 to be spent in retirement.[17] In the presence of a 30 percent tax he must give up $94 of current consumption for the same end.[18] The income tax system nearly triples the amount of current consumption that must be sur-

16. Consider a tax-exempt investment yielding 8 percent and a cost of borrowing of 12 percent. In the absence of tax distortions, it would not make sense to borrow money to buy such a tax-exempt investment, as the investor would lose 4 percent. A taxpayer in the 50 percent bracket can make a profit by such a transaction, however. He can borrow at 12 percent, but his net cost after deducting his interest expenses is only 6 percent. He can make 2 percent on such an investment. The Internal Revenue Code contains provisions designed to discourage such loans, but they are easy to avoid. See Harvey Galper and Eugene Steuerle, "Tax Incentives for Saving," *The Brookings Review*, vol. 2 (Winter 1983), pp. 16–23.

17. For example, in the absence of taxes, the person who earned $1,000 at age thirty could consume $1,000 currently or invest it at 10 percent for thirty-five years, accumulate $28,102, and consume the proceeds. The price of each dollar of retirement consumption, as measured by the amount of first-period consumption that must be surrendered to get $1 of retirement consumption, is $0.0356 (1,000/28,102 = 0.0356).

18. The income tax would reduce the net rate of return from 10 percent to 7 percent. At 7 percent compound interest $94 accumulates to $1,000 after thirty-five years.

rendered for future income security, thereby discouraging the individual from providing for himself.

An Efficient Tax Base. The personal and corporate cash flow taxes would reduce or eliminate most of the investment distortions that would exist under even the most carefully drafted income tax. At the business level, the cash flow tax on corporations would leave the rate of return to investment unchanged relative to pretax levels. Inflation would not alter this result because a deduction for the full cost of an investment would be allowed in the year the investment expenditure is made. In fact, the returns on investments would be taxed only when they were paid out to individuals—as interest, dividends, capital gains, royalties, or other corporate distributions—and consumed, given away, or bequeathed. At that point, they would be fully taxed regardless of the form in which they were realized.

Nor would a cash flow tax distort the timing of consumption. The amount of current consumption that would have to be surrendered to finance each dollar of future consumption would be the same as it would be without taxes.[19] Thus the cash flow tax would not only comport with principles of fairness, but would also terminate tax-induced distortions in savings.

There is some reason to think that adoption of a cash flow tax would lead to an increase in saving by households. Such an increase would be desirable, but the importance of any such effect should not be overestimated. Household saving has run at about 3.5 percent of GNP in recent years.Even if such saving increased by one-third—a decidedly generous estimate—the effect on *national* saving would be a small fraction of the direct and certain effects of eliminating the federal deficit, which is projected to rise to 6 percent of GNP by 1989. The fundamental justification for the cash flow tax should not rest on its problematic effects on saving but rather on its fairness, its ability to reduce distortions in investment and saving, and its ease of administration.

19. If there is a tax of, say, 30 percent, the example in footnote 17 is modified in this way: the person has a choice between consuming $700 currently and investing the $1,000 at 10 percent, realizing $28,102 after thirty-five years, and consuming $19,672 ($28,102 less 30 percent tax). The price per dollar of retirement consumption is again $0.0356 (700/19,762 = 0.0356), the same as in the no-tax case.

Administration

A fair tax will never be truly simple because fairness in taxation requires recognition of individual circumstances. But many of the complexities in the current tax system are the unnecessary result of the inconsistent treatment of capital income. Other complexities come from the numerous individual provisions that cause people to keep records of particular categories of income or expenditures to qualify for one special provision or another.

But even if a personal income tax were applied comprehensively to all income, serious complexities would remain that a cash flow tax would avoid. Under an income tax it is necessary to determine when a person realizes capital income. Because taxpayers can profitably alter the timing of gains and losses, they are driven to engage in complex tax avoidance manipulations. The individual cash flow tax would not encourage such manipulations because the tax occasioned by the sale of an asset of given value would be the same whether there was an accrued gain or loss on it. Yet another advantage of the cash flow tax is that it would sidestep the problem of indexing the tax base, a serious problem under an income tax if inflation runs even as high as 4 or 5 percent per year. The scope for tax shelter investments would also be drastically reduced under the cash flow tax described here.

The cash flow tax, however, would create some new burdens for taxpayers and officials. For example, to calculate their tax base on a cash flow basis, people would have to keep track of all their transactions through qualified accounts. However, after a careful review of the administrative pluses and minuses of taxes like that described here, the Committee on Simplification of the Section on Taxation of the American Bar Association concluded: "If, for example, the prepayment alternative were available only for consumer durables, such as housing, and loan proceeds used to purchase such durables [the approach suggested here], the resulting system might be substantially simpler than even that which could be attained under a comprehensive income tax."[20]

20. "Complexity and the Personal Consumption Tax," *Tax Lawyer*, vol. 35 (Winter 1981–82), p. 426.

Special Problems

The program set forth here advances the goals of fairness, efficiency, and administrative simplicity described above. There are, however, a number of problems to be resolved.

Transition

If nothing were done to ease the transition, the switch to a cash flow tax would be unfair to people who had accumulated assets out of previously taxed income. This problem would be most serious for older workers and retirees, who without special transition rules would be taxed a second time when those assets were consumed.

In dealing with the transition, one faces a trade-off between simplicity and individualized treatment. If simplicity is a paramount goal, most taxpayers would be helped by allowing everyone over a particular age exemptions for some amount of consumption. If individualized treatment is considered more important, each household could calculate the aggregate cost of all assets accumulated from savings out of previously taxed income ("basis" in current tax law) and claim an exemption spread over a number of years for consumption until that aggregate cost had been recovered tax free.

Special transition rules would also be necessary to deal with existing capital and debt. Firms should be allowed to write off over a period of time all capital in existence at the time the new tax rules take effect. They should also be required to take outstanding debt into the tax base according to a fixed schedule, although deductions for repayments of principal and interest on debt outstanding would be allowed.

Current Tax Preferences

Existing deductions, exclusions, and credits that do not help in measuring ability to pay should not be transferred en masse to the new system, as the result would be a system just as unfair, distorting, and complex as the present one. We understand the desire to accord favored treatment to some sources or uses of income. In such cases, however, the use of direct governmental expenditures or tax credits would be preferable to deductions as a means of achieving the desired end. Although arguments can be advanced for encouraging people to consume particular goods, the use of tax deductions and exclusions to convey such encouragement both complicates the system and is unlikely to establish the best pattern of subsidies. Since the benefits that taxpayers enjoy from exclusions and deductions are proportional to their marginal tax rates, the largest subsidies accrue to those with the most income.

A few examples illustrate these points. The tax code currently excludes from taxable income employer-provided health care and allows individual deductions for the excess of medical outlays over 5 percent of income. The value of employer-provided health care should be included in the cash flow tax base, as these outlays support household consumption. However, because extraordinary medical expenses are an involuntary consequence of serious illness and directly reduce the resources that the taxpayers can use at their discretion, a deduction for extraordinary medical outlays should be retained.

If encouragement of charitable giving is regarded as important enough to merit exceptional tax treatment, a tax credit, rather than a deduction, should be used. A credit would provide equal encouragement to all taxpayers; a deduction provides greatest encouragement to giving by people in the highest tax brackets.

Housing

The current tax law treats investments in owner-occupied housing more favorably than other investments. Owners are not required to count the rental value of their own houses in their income, but they are allowed to claim deductions for mortgage interest and property taxes. Taxation of owner-occupied housing would also pose unique problems under the cash flow tax. To deal with these problems, some analysts have suggested excluding all aspects of the purchase of a home from the tax system. That is, no deduction would be given for the investment, and neither the proceeds of mortgages nor their repayments would have any effect on tax. Only the amounts withdrawn from qualified accounts for down payments would be subject to tax.

This approach simplifies the tax treatment of housing, but raises other problems. The size of down payments could cause large bulges in consumption and corresponding bulges in tax. This problem could be solved by averaging, that is, by including in current consumption some fixed share of the down payment, say 10 percent each year for ten years.[21]

Averaging

As an additional averaging device, households might be allowed to carry outstanding loans up to some dollar limit, say $20,000, without being taxed on such borrowing. Of course, deductions for interest and principal on such tax-free borrowing would be disallowed. This provision would enable taxpayers to make some debt-financed outlays without incurring an immediate tax liability. The denial of deductibility for payments of interest and principal has the effect of shifting the tax liability to the future with interest. The amount of borrowing would be subject to a cap in order to limit possible manipulation between tax-free borrowing and tax-preferred saving.

Alternative Approaches to Tax Reform

We believe that a cash flow tax on individuals and corporations would go farther toward achieving the goals outlined in this chapter than any other system. It would impose tax burdens based on each person's lifetime command over resources. It would terminate the capricious variation in business

21. Alternatively, the purchase of a house could be treated like any other investment, but owner-occupants could be required to include in each year's tax base a practical approximation of the gross rental stream. The approximation would be based on guideline percentages adjusted for changes in gross rents and applied to the purchase price of the house. This procedure would yield a set of calculated gross rents designed to provide a fair rate of return on the value of the asset. The value of the flows discounted at that rate of return would just equal the initial deduction for the price paid for the house. Under this approach, a deduction would be given for the purchase price, the proceeds of mortgages and funds withdrawn from qualified accounts would be included in current receipts, and loan amortization would be fully deductible.

tax rates under present law, thereby reducing the scope for tax avoidance through tax shelters. It would ease compliance for those who face the greatest difficulty in determining their tax liabilities under current law.

This approach is, of course, not the only approach to tax reform. Two other widely discussed changes—comprehensive income tax reform and the value-added tax—would permit considerable progress to be made toward one or more of the goals of improving fairness, promoting economic efficiency, and facilitating administration.[22]

Comprehensive Income Tax Reform

Among the many proposals advanced in recent years to tax income comprehensively, draft legislation introduced in 1983 by Senator Bill Bradley, Democrat of New Jersey, and Representative Richard Gephardt, Democrat of Missouri, is currently the most prominent. This proposal would not only broaden the income tax base, but would also change its structure.[23] It would move the tax system toward the goal of taxing annual economic income. This bill would eliminate the 60 percent exclusion for long-term capital gains. It would repeal or limit many tax credits, lengthen the depreciable lives of most investments, include certain government transfer payments in the tax base, repeal deductions for state and local taxes other than income and property taxes, and end the exclusion of

22. The "flat-tax" proposal of Robert Hall and Alvin Rabushka makes as much progress toward promoting economic efficiency and administration as the system presented here. But it sacrifices the objective of fairness (because income that is not consumed is never taxed), and its flat rate causes major alterations in the distribution of tax burdens. Despite claims to the contrary by Hall and Rabushka, their proposal would greatly reduce tax burdens for high-income households and increase them for middle- and lower-middle-income households. See Hall and Rabushka, *Low Tax, Simple Tax, Flat Tax.* The same holds true for other flat-tax proposals. For general analysis, see Joseph A. Minarik, "The Future of the Individual Income Tax," *National Tax Journal,* vol. 35 (September 1982), pp. 236–41; and Joseph A. Pechman and John Karl Scholtz, "Comprehensive Income Taxation and Rate Reduction," *Tax Notes,* vol. 17 (October 11, 1982), pp. 83–93 (Brookings Reprint 390).

23. S. 1421, Fair Tax Act of 1983. See *Congressional Record,* daily edition (June 8, 1983), pp. S7836–57. Other bills introduced in Congress to broaden the tax base and lower rates include S. 1040 by Sen. Dan Quayle, Republican of Indiana, and S. 557 by Sen. Dennis DeConcini, Democrat of Arizona (the latter based on the Hall-Rabushka proposal).

certain fringe benefits, including employer-purchased health insurance.

These and other measures to broaden the tax base would permit the same revenues to be collected as under current law with three rate brackets of 14, 26, and 30 percent.[24] About 80 percent of all taxpayers would be subject to the bottom rate of 14 percent.[25] Despite the reduction in the number of brackets, this proposal would have little overall effect on the distribution of individual tax burdens by broad income classes because the revenue-increasing effects of base broadening would be offset by reductions in tax rates.

At the corporate level, the proposal would repeal the investment tax credit and make a number of other changes that would broaden the tax base. Again a reduction of the tax rate from the current level of 46 percent to 30 percent, the same as the top-bracket rate applicable to individuals, would offset the revenue effects of base broadening.

If the Bradley-Gephardt tax base were to be used to reach the revenue targets presented in this book, however, the rates contained in their bill would have to be increased by about 19 percent. The resulting rate structure would be 17 percent for the lowest bracket, 31 percent for the middle bracket, and 36 percent for the top bracket.

The Bradley-Gephardt proposal, or other measures to broaden the income tax base, would achieve a number of important reforms. By lowering the number of favored sources or uses of income, these changes would simplify the tax law and reduce tax-induced distortions. In addition, they would enable a given amount of revenue to be collected with lower rates than is possible under current law. This change also greatly lessens both the distortions generated by any special provisions that remain and the incentives to conceal or shelter income.

24. Personal exemptions would be set at $1,600 per taxpayer. In addition, there would be a zero-bracket amount of $3,000 for single persons and $6,000 for others. Personal exemptions and itemized deductions would apply only against the 14 percent rate; in other words, the tax above 14 percent would fall on income with no allowance for such deductions.

25. The 14 percent bracket would apply to the first $40,000 of taxable income of joint filers; the 26 percent rate would apply to the next $25,000 of income; and the 30 percent rate would apply to taxable income over $65,000. The comparable brackets for single returns would be up to $25,000, $25,000 to $37,500, and over $37,500.

However, the Bradley-Gephardt proposal also contains a number of dubious elements. It would repeal bracket indexing, which would cause inflation to push taxpayers into higher tax brackets. It would allow deductions for catastrophic medical expenses (defined as expenditures greater than 10 percent of income) only at the 14 percent rate.

More important, it cannot correct certain problems inherent in any income tax. First, it does not deal with inflation-related distortions in the tax base.[26] Second, the Bradley-Gephardt proposal would impose different personal taxes on people with equal lifetime income patterns. The annual taxation of realized capital income, whether or not it is consumed, would continue to distort individual saving decisions and encourage the socially unproductive conversion of labor or capital income into capital gains. To be sure, the bill's proposed repeal of the exclusion of 60 percent of long-term capital gains would reduce this incentive somewhat. But since most capital gains are never taxed, the contribution of this provision to simplification and fairness is limited.[27] Finally, although the Bradley-Gephardt bill holds out smaller promise of improvements in fairness, efficiency, and simplification than the proposal put forward here, it would entail equally far-reaching changes in the tax laws.

Value-Added Tax

For many years the value-added tax has had enough support to remain under almost continual discussion, but it has never come close to enactment. The value-added tax is a sales tax levied at each stage of production on "value added," the difference between total sales proceeds and the cost of goods and services purchased from other firms. The most frequently

26. The depreciation deduction, for example, would yield an accurate measure of capital income only at a discount rate of 10 percent, a level customarily associated with inflation of about 7 percent. At higher or lower rates of inflation, the depreciation deduction would unevenly tax capital income, as does current law.

27. An additional change that would go further toward reducing the incentives to convert ordinary income into capital gains would be constructive realization of capital gains at death. Even this rule would continue the major advantage of deferral and consequently preserve a large incentive to convert ordinary income into capital gains. The Bradley-Gephardt proposal does not call for this change.

discussed form of the value-added tax permits firms to deduct immediately the cost of all investments. As a result, a comprehensive value-added tax may be shown to be equivalent to a tax on all consumption. It has the same economic effects as a truly comprehensive retail sales tax.

Part of the attraction of the value-added tax is its widespread use in the European Economic Community, where it accounts for about one-sixth of total government revenues.[28] No country now imposes a comprehensive value-added tax, however, and all the proposals advanced in the United States would excuse a large share of consumption from the tax. Two factors explain the attraction of a *partial* value-added tax. The first concerns the distributional effects of a comprehensive value-added tax. Such a tax would be proportional with respect to consumption, but regressive with respect to annual income (because the proportion of income that is saved rises with income) and with respect to lifetime resources or endowments (because it would not reach bequests, which rise more than proportionately with income). Most countries have sought to reduce this regressivity by excusing from full taxation those goods on which low-income families spend larger-than-average shares of their incomes. This policy has made the value-added tax roughly proportional with respect to annual income in some countries.

Second, a truly comprehensive value-added tax would be very hard to administer because it would be necessary to tax such activities as services of financial institutions and nonprofit organizations and the imputed rental services of owner-occupied housing and other durable consumer goods. To make the tax easier to administer, no existing value-added tax reaches all consumption. While the decision not to tax these goods simplifies administration, the imposition of different rates of tax on different classes of commodities adds to administrative complexity.

Most proposals for a value-added tax in the United States have suggested taxing roughly 50 percent of all consumption. If such consumption were taxed at a uniform rate, a value-

28. Henry J. Aaron, ed., *The Value-Added Tax: Lessons from Europe* (Brookings Institution, 1981), p. 14.

added tax would yield about $18 billion for each percentage point in 1989. A tax of 8 percent would increase net revenues by the $108 billion required to reach the revenue target in table 1-1.[29]

Not all of the proceeds of a value-added tax would be available to reduce the deficit, however, unless Congress were prepared to impose significant tax burdens on economic groups now regarded as too poor to pay income taxes.[30] It would be possible to prevent such a shift of taxes to the poor by providing refundable personal income tax credits. But these credits would require the filing of tax returns by millions of low-income people who are not now required to file tax returns. The result would be increases in the cost of income tax administration and compliance. Furthermore, payment of such rebates would increase the rates necessary to yield sufficient revenue to meet revenue targets.

A high-rate value-added tax would create at least one serious political problem. In the view of many, it would hinder state and local governments from raising retail sales taxes. It would be possible to impose a value-added tax at rates high enough not only to meet federal revenue goals, but also to permit the federal government to "buy-out" the retail sales taxes of states and localities. Under such a scheme a portion of tax proceeds would be used to provide grants to states, in return for which the states would give up retail sales taxation. But it is unlikely that the states would willingly suffer the loss of fiscal autonomy entailed in such a swap.

By itself the value-added tax would do nothing to correct the existing shortcomings of the personal and corporation income taxes. Enactment of the value-added tax would not relieve Congress from the obligation to reform personal and corporation income taxes if it wanted to correct the unfairness, distortion, and complexity arising under the present tax system.

29. This rate must be set to yield $108 billion after allowing for the offset in income tax collections due to the increased gap between output at market prices and income at factor cost occasioned by the value-added tax.

30. Some low-income earners now actually receive subsidies, as they pay little or no income tax and qualify for the earned-income tax credit, a payment based on earnings provided to many persons with earned income below $10,000 dollars per year.

These problems can be dealt with only by changes in the personal and corporation income taxes themselves. The value-added tax can raise a lot of revenue—and it may have certain desirable characteristics—but it cannot achieve a fair, efficient, or simple tax system unless it is combined with direct reforms of personal and business taxes.

Conclusion

To advance the national economic goals emphasized through-out this book, tax revenues must be raised and the tax system must be reformed to improve its equity and to reduce tax-created distortions of economic decisions. The tax system should be simplified, both to reduce costs of compliance and enforcement and to enable taxpayers to understand the system by which they pay for public services. The tax structure advanced here would accomplish these goals.

Fairness would be achieved by taxing equally those with equal cash flows. Efficiency would be promoted by reducing tax-related distortions of investment and saving. Simplicity would be advanced by use of a cash flow tax base that eliminates the need to calculate depreciation and capital gains and that levies taxes of equal present value whenever capital income is consumed or transferred.

One caution must be stressed. A failure to adopt certain key elements of this proposal would seriously compromise the achievement of these goals. In particular, overly large exemptions for transfers by gift or at death would undermine the fairness of the cash flow tax. Such excessive exemptions would result in very different tax burdens on equally situated taxpayers. Also, the adoption of special provisions leading to uneven taxation of various categories of investment would erode the gains in efficiency and simplicity from uniform treatment of investment.

If gifts and bequests are not included in the cash flow tax base or if substantial variations in the treatment of alternative investments occur, a wholly different approach to tax reform may well be preferable. With an excessive exemption of bequests or gifts, the continued annual taxation of capital income as realized would hold considerable attraction as the only device (other than a freestanding wealth tax) for reaching income from inherited accumulations of wealth.

The current income tax system has gone astray in large measure because it has ceased to reflect any coherent unifying principle. The income tax at all times has suffered from shortcomings inherent in the way it treats capital income. But the mélange of inconsistent principles in various aspects of the income tax has produced absurd complexity and unintended and indefensible distortions. A major increase in revenue should not be obtained from this distorted tax base. Thorough reform is vital. And reform can be accomplished only if the goals of fairness, efficiency, and ease of administration are kept resolutely in mind.

6

Adjusting to Economic Change

IN PREVIOUS chapters we have argued that a major shift in macroeconomic policy would improve the chances for sustained economic growth and enhance U.S. competitiveness in world markets. Reducing the deficit rapidly and bringing interest rates down would encourage the saving and investment needed for long-run growth and improve the competitive position of U.S. industry by reducing the value of the dollar in foreign exchange markets. But suppose that these policies were successfully implemented, that the economy was expanding at an annual 4 percent real rate of growth, and that the dollar was declining toward its 1980 level. Would this country not still have declining industries, distressed regions, and dislocated workers? Would it not still be at a disadvantage in world trade, especially in competing with countries that subsidize their industries and engage in unfair trade practices?

In this chapter we attempt to sort out the extent to which the structural and trade-related problems of U.S. industry result from slow growth, recession, and unfavorable exchange rates and what problems would remain if these were alleviated. Our basic finding is that while sustained growth and more favorable exchange rates would not eliminate structural and trade problems entirely, they would reduce them to manageable proportions. We see no evidence that the United States is

Robert Z. Lawrence, Lawrence B. Krause, Robert H. Meyer, and Linda Cohen undertook primary responsibility for drafting this chapter.

deindustrializing, that structural change is accelerating, or that this country is suffering from some fundamental disadvantage in world trade.

But even in a growing economy, the transfer of people and resources from less productive to more productive sectors will pose painful problems for some workers, companies, and communities, and the government will be pressured to retard these painful changes through protectionism and other measures. We believe policy should be designed to foster growth and to aid the victims of change in ways that help them adjust to it, not avoid it. The chapter thus offers suggestions for ways of making economic policy more visible, improving trade policy, helping dislocated workers, and encouraging research and development.

What Is Happening to U.S. Manufacturing?

The past few years have been extremely difficult for U.S. manufacturing. In the face of two major recessions, manufacturing employment fell from 21 million in 1979 to 18.2 million in December 1982. The slump reduced employment in both high-technology and basic industries and was particularly severe in the automobile and steel industries. Although the manufacturing sector has enjoyed a vigorous recovery since December 1982, employment in manufacturing stood at just 19.5 million in March 1984—well below its 1979 level. Moreover, manufacturers have had continuing difficulty selling products abroad and competing with imports. In 1983 the U.S. trade deficit in manufactured products was $31 billion; the figure for 1984 will likely be higher.

Although manufacturing accounts for only about one-fifth of total employment, it is often considered the fulcrum of a modern economy, an important source of jobs and high wages, the major locus of productivity growth, the center of vital regional economies, and a crucial contributor to national defense. Thus in formulating economic policy it is important to consider whether economic recovery and more favorable exchange rates can restore manufacturing activity to previous levels and increase net manufactured exports, or whether the recent difficulties of manufacturers reflect a more basic long-term decline in manufacturing and an inability to compete effectively in world markets. Even if manufacturing recovers in the aggregate, will shifts in the industrial structure cause serious mismatches between workers and jobs?

Recent Experience in the Manufacturing Sector

In 1980–82, for the first time in postwar history, employment in U.S. manufacturing fell for three consecutive years. The 10.4 percent decline over this period was the largest since 1946. The slump was also unusual because of the important role played by international trade imbalances. But these developments were the predictable effects of two recessions and the strong dollar. Evidence indicates that in a year in which GNP fails to grow, manufacturing employment will decline 3.7 percent.[1] In 1982, GNP was just 0.4 percent higher than in 1979, and the 10.4 percent decline in employment in manufacturing between 1979 and 1982 was close to the expected 10.6 percent decline. Between the fourth quarter of 1982 and the fourth quarter of 1983, manufacturing employment increased by 5 percent, which was again close to the 4.4 percent that would have been expected given the 6 percent rise in GNP during this period.

A substantial share of the decline in manufacturing employment between 1980 and 1982 was due to the loss of jobs related to manufactured exports: their number alone fell by 0.5 million.[2] When the dollar soared in 1980 and continued to strengthen in 1981 and 1982, U.S. companies were priced out of world markets. Operating with lags that have their most powerful impact between eighteen and thirty months, the trade balance for manufactured goods declined dramatically. Econometric evidence confirms that the erosion in U.S trade performance was the predictable result of the global recession and the appreciation of the dollar.

1. The regression of the annual percentage change in GNP (G) on manufacturing employment (E) as in $E = -3.7 + 1.35\ G$. (t-statistics in parentheses)
$$(3.9)\quad (5.9)$$
2. Robert Z. Lawrence, "Is Trade Deindustralizing America? A Medium-Term Perspective," *Brookings Papers on Economic Activity, 1:1983*, p. 150. (Hereafter *BPEA*.)

The ability of manufacturing employment and output to maintain their previous relationship to GNP despite increases in unemployment caused by trade imbalances suggests that there are otfsetting sources of strength in the demand for U.S manufactured products. A major source of that strength was a $28.7 billion increase in military procurement from 1980 to 1983. In addition, particularly in 1983, investment in equipment was stronger than in a normal recovery.[3] Thus what has happened recently to U.S. manufacturing is a predictable result of recession and a strong currency. Recent experience does not suggest that new structural forces are operating to reduce the output of U.S. manufacturing.

Nor does experience during the 1970s. The share of manufacturing employment in total employment has been declining for a long time in the United States, as it has in other advanced countries, reflecting increasing consumer preference for services and greater manufacturing productivity. The absolute number of jobs in manufacturing, however, has continued to increase modestly in the United States, although manufacturing employment declined in the same period in other major manufacturing countries (see table 6-1).

Slow growth in manufacturing output was a worldwide phenomenon in the 1970s, reflecting slow overall economic growth. U.S. production of manufactured goods grew about as rapidly as GNP from 1950 to 1973, but the increase in industrial production slowed more than GNP growth from 1973 to 1980. However, econometric evidence suggests that, given the slow growth in GNP, manufacturing output was almost exactly what should have been expected. Thus slow demand was the reason for the relatively slow growth. Other countries experienced a similar slackening in demand, and the increase in U.S. manufacturing output since 1973 has been about the same as the average of all industrial countries.

The evidence from the 1970s also contradicts any contention that the United States has been neglecting its manufacturing sector by failing to invest in capital stock or in research and development. As table 6-1 shows, U.S. investment in physical

3. See *Survey of Current Business,* vol. 64 (January 1984), p. 7.

Table 6-1. *U.S. and Foreign Manufacturing Performance, Selected Years, 1960–81*

Average annual growth rates unless otherwise indicated

Item	United States	Japan	Germany	Europe
Inputs				
Capital stock				
1960–73	3.1	12.8[a]	6.5	5.3[b]
1973–76	3.5	6.7	2.3	3.2[b]
1976–80	4.8	4.6	2.0	2.5[b]
Employment (total hours)				
1960–73	1.6	2.3	−0.3	n.a.
1973–80	0.5	−0.8	−2.8	n.a.
Percentage change in employment share				
High-growth industries,[c] 1973–79	8.9	0.6	3.0	n.a.
Low-growth industries,[c] 1973–79	−5.9	−6.4	−9.2	n.a.
Share of output spent on all R&D, 1977	6.5	3.7	4.0	n.a.
Share of output spent on private R&D, 1977	4.4	3.6	3.4	n.a.
Productivity				
Output per worker hour				
1960–73	3.4	10.5	5.5	n.a.
1973–80	1.3	6.7	4.6	n.a.
Level of labor productivity, 1980				
(United States = 100)	100.0	84.0	78.3	n.a.
Output				
Production				
1960–73	5.0	13.0	5.2	n.a.
1973–80	1.8	5.7	1.6	1.6
Trade				
Share of world exports of manufactures				
1960	22.8	6.5	18.2	65.8
1973	16.4	13.1	20.9	67.2
1980	16.4	11.9	19.8	66.1
1981	18.1	14.5	18.7	61.4

Sources: Data on growth in manufacturing capital stock are from Organization for Economic Cooperation and Development, *Flows and Stocks of Fixed Capital, 1955–1980* (Paris: OECD, 1983); data on growth in manufacturing employment, production, and labor productivity are from Bureau of Labor Statistics, "International Comparison of Manufacturing Productivity and Labor Trends," press release, USDL 83-248, May 26, 1983; data on total and private R&D spending in manufacturing are from OECD, *OECD Science and Technology Indicators: Resources Devoted to R&D* (Paris: OECD, 1984), p. 54; data on exports of manufactures are from United Nations, *Monthly Bulletin of Statistics,* various issues; data on level of manufacturing labor productivity are from A. D. Roy, "Labor Productivity in 1980: An International Comparison," *National Institute Economic Review,* no. 101 (August 1982), p. 29.

n.a. Not available.

a. Data for 1964–73.

b. Capital stock for Europe is a weighted average of French, German, and British stock. For weights in 1975, see OECD, *Main Economic Indicators, January 1984* (Paris: OECD, 1984).

c. High-growth industries include industrial chemicals, other chemical products, plastic products, machinery, electrical machinery, and professional goods. Low-growth industries include textiles, apparel, leather, footwear, wood products, furniture, iron and steel, nonferrous metals, metal products, and shipbuilding. See Robert Z. Lawrence, *Can America Compete?* (Brookings Institution, 1984), p. 32.

capital and R&D in manufacturing compared favorably both
with historical rates and with other major industrial countries.
From 1960 to 1973 the net capital stock in U.S. manufacturing
grew at an annual rate of 3.1 percent; from 1973 to 1980,
however, it averaged an annual growth rate of 4.2 percent.
The increase since 1973 has exceeded that in Germany, France,
Sweden, and the United Kingdom. Between 1975 and 1980
manufacturing capital stock grew at similar rates in the United
States and Japan.[4] The growth rate in real spending on R&D
in U.S. manufacturing has also accelerated since 1973. From
1960 to 1972 real spending for R&D grew at an annual rate of
1.9 percent; from 1972 to 1979 it averaged 2.4 percent per year.[5]
R&D spending was 6.5 percent of net output in manufacturing
in 1977; Germany managed only 4.0 percent and Japan 3.7
percent. And even though the U.S. manufacturing labor force
is two-thirds that of Japan, Germany, France, and the United
Kingdom combined, it employs about 30 percent more scientists
and engineers in R&D.[6]

The evidence from the 1970s also indicates that U.S. manufactures, aided by the falling value of the dollar, competed
successfully in world markets despite emerging competition
from developing countries and Japan, increased government
trade intervention and protection in Europe, and lagging U.S.
productivity growth. Indeed, between 1973 and 1980 the post–
World War II decline in the U.S. share of world trade in
manufactured goods was arrested. The favorable balance of
trade in manufactured goods increased from nearly zero to
$18.3 billion. The favorable trade balance in high-technology
industries grew especially rapidly, more than offsetting declines
in the trade balance for "low-technology" manufacturing products.[7] From 1973 to 1980 foreign trade provided a net addition

4. Organization for Economic Cooperation and Development, *Flows and Stocks of Fixed Capital* (Paris: OECD, 1983).

5. OECD, *Science and Technology Indicators: Resources Devoted to R&D* (Paris: OECD, 1984), pp. 54, 112.

6. See Rolf Piekarz, Eleanor Thomas, and Donna Jennings, "International Comparison of Research and Development Expenditures," paper prepared for the Conference on International Comparisons of Productivity and Causes of the Slowdown, Washington, D.C.: American Enterprise Institute for Public Policy Research, September 30 and October 1, 1982.

7. National Science Foundation, *Science Indicators, 1980* (Government Printing Office, 1981), p. 32.

to production and jobs in U.S. manufacturing and added jobs in thirty-eight of the fifty-two U.S. industries.

One lesson of the 1970s is that competition from developing countries need not harm U.S. manufacturing exports as a whole, although it may change the mix. Developing countries can buy the latest equipment and then use their lower-paid workers to make some standardized products more cheaply than they can be produced in developed countries. But the machines that incorporate the latest equipment are built in developed countries. Indeed, U.S. concentration on exporting machinery enabled its exports of manufactured goods to oil-importing developing countries to grow more rapidly than those of Japan from 1973 to 1980.[8]

The growth in U.S. productivity was slower in the 1970s than it was for other industrial countries, but U.S. productivity levels in manufacturing remain the highest in the world (see table 6-1). And slower productivity growth, while damaging to the U.S. standard of living, need not reduce competitiveness in international markets. Faster productivity growth abroad may be diverted into higher wages and profits rather than show up in lower prices. And even if, in foreign currencies, foreign prices do not rise as much as U.S. prices, a more favorable exchange rate for exports could offset the differential as it did in the 1970s.

The Shift to High-Technology Industries

In the 1970s, employment in high-technology industries—those with a relatively high proportion of spending on R&D—grew while jobs in low-technology industries declined. This type of structural shift can cause serious dislocations of workers if the jobs gained are substantially different in kind from the jobs lost, even if total employment is unchanged. The stereotypical example of such shifts compares the computer industry with the steel and automobile industries. As table 6-2 shows, these sectors have markedly different characteristics. The steel and automobile industries employ high proportions of minor-

8. General Agreement on Tariffs and Trade, *International Trade, 1981–82* (Geneva: GATT, 1982).

Table 6-2. *Some Characteristics of U.S. High- and Low-Technology Industries during the Past Two Decades*[a]

Item	High-technology industry	Low-technology industry	Computers	Automobiles	Steel
Employees (thousands)[b]	6,513.4	13,771.6	354.2	788.8	428.4
Black employees (percent)[c]	5.3	9.7	4.1	13.5	13.0
Women employees (percent)[b]	30.7	33.2	35.9	14.0	6.9
Production workers (percent)[b]	62.1	74.3	40.0	72.9	77.5
Employees covered by collective bargaining (percent)[d]					
All workers	38.9	49.0	11.0	72.0	77.0
Production workers	58.2	61.5	15.0	98.0	98.0
Median number of school years completed[c]	12.5	11.6	13.7	12.1	12.0
Median age in years[c]	38.9	40.3	32.6	39.3	43.7
Work force stability (percent of workers employed 50–52 weeks)[c]	76.8	70.4	79.5	70.9	77.8
Average hourly wage of production workers (dollars)[b]	7.62	7.12	6.73	9.85	11.84
Average annual compensation of all workers (dollars)[b]	22,300	18,800	23,000	30,300	34,100
Capital-labor ratio (dollars)[b]	23,700	30,790	21,600	40,200	93,400
Labor's share (percent)[b]	51.9	50.3	47.7	70.8	73.8
Large-plant percentage[e]	41.4	23.6	58.5	71.5	89.4
Concentration ratio (percent)[e]	42.8	36.4	44.0	82.0	45.0
Allocation of employment by geographical census regions (percent)[f]					
Middle Atlantic	21.4	20.5	18.6	8.8	32.9
New England	10.0	6.6	12.1	1.2	0.4
East North Central	28.8	24.7	4.6	65.9	42.7
West North Central	6.2	6.0	14.0	6.7	1.3
South	19.6	32.1	13.4	11.5	16.5
West	14.0	10.1	37.3	6.0	6.1

Sources: Annual compensation, capital-labor ratio, and share of labor are from U.S. Bureau of the Census, *1980 Annual Survey of Manufactures*, M80 (A5)-5 (September 1982); race, school years, age, and work force stability are from Bureau of the Census, *1970 Census of Population* (Government Printing Office, 1973); concentration ratios and regional employment are from Bureau of the Census, *1972 Census of Manufactures* (GPO, 1975) and *1977 Census of Manufactures* (GPO, 1981), respectively; data on total employment, women, production workers, and average wages are from Bureau of Labor Statistics, *Employment and Earnings*, various issues; union coverage is from Richard B. Freeman and James L. Medoff, "New Estimates of Private Sector Unionism in the United States," *Industrial and Labor Relations Review*, vol. 32 (January 1979), pp. 143–74.

a. The characteristics of high- and low-technology industries are based on a sample of three-digit 1970 census code industries that employed 85 percent of the employees in manufacturing in 1980. Employment figures for high- and low-technology industries are from total manufacturing data. The Standard Industrial Classification codes for computers, automobiles, and steel are 3573, 371, and 3312, respectively.

b. In 1980. Annual compensation includes social security and benefits. The capital-labor ratio is the gross book value of depreciable assets divided by employment. Labor's share is total employee compensation divided by value added.

c. In 1970. To derive median school years and median age we computed the weighted average (by number of employees) of the medians of men and women in the three-digit 1970 census-code industries.

d. From surveys of the 1968–72 period.

e. In 1977. The concentration ratio is the weighted average of the percent of output produced by the four largest companies in each four-digit Standard Industrial Classification industry. The large-plant percentage is the percent of employees in establishments with 1,000 or more workers.

f. In 1972; Bureau of Census regions.

ities, low proportions of women, and high proportions of production workers. They are highly unionized, their workers have average educational levels but earn wages much higher than the manufacturing average, and they have a high proportion of large plants concentrated in the Middle Atlantic and the East North Central regions.

In the computer industry the work force has considerably more white, female, educated, and young workers. The industry is much less unionized, pays less than the average wage in manufacturing, and is heavily concentrated in the West. Thus if adjusting to structural change meant hiring automobile workers to build computers, as conventional wisdom appears to presume, the adjustment would be considerable. But fortunately these industries do not accurately represent the difference between high- and low-technology manufacturing. Indeed, differences in regional location and occupational characteristics between high- and low-technology workers are surprisingly small (see table 6-2).

There is no evidence that the pace of structural change in the mix of employment is accelerating: the degree of change in the 1970s was no greater than in the 1950s and 1960s,[9] and for most industries the pace in the 1970s was not overwhelming. Taken together, employment in low-technology industries fell at an annual average rate of 0.03 percent in the 1970s; the decline from the cyclical peak in 1973 through the slacker conditions in 1980 averaged 0.82 percent per year. In fact, the employment loss due to the shift in structural change over the entire decade of the 1970s was considerably smaller than the loss in one year of a major recession. For example, from 1973 to 1975 employment in low-technology sectors fell at an annual average rate of 5.6 percent, and from 1979 to 1982 the drop averaged 4.7 percent per year.

In some industries the pace of decline was more rapid, but voluntary attrition probably absorbed the gradual decline in employment so that major layoffs were unnecessary. The problem, of course, is that employment declines often result in the closing of whole plants rather than gradual declines in many different plants.

---

9. Robert Z. Lawrence, *Can America Compete?* (Brookings Institution, 1984), p. 52.

Unfortunately, many declining industries possess character-istics that exacerbate the adverse consequences of structural change. Four of the five major industries with the slowest employment growth (tobacco, automobiles, primary metals, and textiles) are among those that have the largest plants and are therefore important to the economic health of the regions in which they are located. Workers in such declining industries as steel and automobiles earn wage premiums because of strong unions. They have, therefore, considerable financial incentive to resist structural change, an incentive that can only be mitigated by effective programs, such as those discussed later in this chapter, to help them adjust.

The Future

It is widely believed that a high proportion of the jobs lost in manufacturing will not return with economic recovery, but there is no evidence that this is true. Between November 1982 and December 1983 employment in U.S. manufacturing in-creased by 1 million or about 5.5 percent. The bulk of the rise came in low-technology employment. If the economy were to sustain a 4.0 percent average growth rate between 1983 and 1989, employment in high- and low-technology manufacturing would grow at annual average rates of 3.5 and 2.0 percent, respectively. If the dollar were to return about halfway to its 1980 value, an additional 66 million jobs (or a 3.5 percent growth in manufacturing jobs in 1983) could be generated. Thus, given reasonable economic expansion and international price competitiveness, manufacturing employment should re-turn to its 1979 level by 1987 and grow moderately for the balance of the decade. Structural shifts would continue but would not create unmanageable problems.

Dislocated Workers

A dynamic, growing economy requires that labor, capital, and natural resources flow to their most productive use. As new companies and new industries emerge, others decline and their work forces become available for more productive tasks.

Within the last thirty-five years this process has led to a 50 percent real increase in hourly wages and more than a doubling of real per capita consumption. The transition from one job to the next can impose steep costs on some workers, however, and public action is needed to speed their adjustment to structural changes.

The Birth and Death of Jobs

During the 1970s employment grew by 26 percent as more than 20 million net new jobs were added to the economy, and despite a severe recession, it grew by 1.5 million from 1980 to 1983. The national birthrate of jobs has thus significantly exceeded their death rate. The number of workers who lose their jobs because of economic change, however, could be large even if net employment is rising. Technological change, shifts in the composition of demand, and changing international trade patterns are a continual source of job births and deaths. However, not all job deaths result in unemployment. A worker may find another job quickly, accept a transfer within his company, or retire or otherwise voluntarily leave the labor force. And not all unemployment is a result of job disappearance; some workers are temporarily laid off, quit their previous job, or are looking for their first job since entering or reentering the labor force. Permanent layoffs generally represent between 25 and 40 percent of all unemployment (see table 6-3).

Unemployment Caused by Permanent Layoffs

The proportion of the labor force unemployed because of permanent layoffs varies substantially over the business cycle (see table 6-3). At the peak of the business cycle in 1979 about 1.7 percent of the labor force was unemployed because of permanent layoffs (out of a total unemployment rate of 5.8 percent). The proportion rose to 4.0 percent (with total unemployment at 9.6 percent) in 1983, while the average duration of unemployment increased from 13.1 weeks to 19.0 weeks. We estimate that in 1982 and 1983 almost 11 percent of the labor

Table 6-3. *The Duration of Unemployment, Annual Incidence of Unemployment, and Unemployment Rates by Reason for Unemployment, 1968–86*

Year	Estimate of duration of unemployment for workers permanently laid off (weeks)[a]	Estimate of annual incidence of unemployment due to permanent layoffs[b]	Unemployment rates				
			Permanent layoffs[c]	Temporary layoffs[c]	Quits[c]	Entry/reentry[c]	Total civilian unemployment rate[c]
1968	10.1	4.6	0.9	0.4	0.6	1.7	3.6
1969	9.4	4.4	0.8	0.4	0.5	1.7	3.4
1970	11.1	6.6	1.4	0.8	0.7	2.1	5.0
1971	14.8	6.7	1.9	0.9	0.7	2.5	6.0
1972	15.2	6.2	1.8	0.7	0.7	2.5	4.9
1973	12.5	5.8	1.4	0.5	0.8	2.2	4.9
1974	12.3	6.7	1.6	0.8	0.8	2.3	5.5
1975	17.6	8.6	2.9	1.8	0.9	2.9	8.5
1976	19.4	7.2	2.7	1.1	0.9	2.9	7.6
1977	17.4	6.9	2.3	0.9	0.9	3.0	7.1
1978	14.2	6.6	1.8	0.7	0.9	2.7	6.1
1979	13.1	6.8	1.7	0.8	0.8	2.5	5.8
1980	11.4	10.5	2.3	1.4	0.8	2.6	7.1
1981	16.2	8.3	2.6	1.3	0.9	2.8	7.6
1982	17.7	11.1	3.8	1.9	0.8	3.2	9.7
1983	19.0	11.0	4.0	1.6	0.7	3.3	9.6
1984[d]	15.4	8.8	2.6	n.a.	n.a.	n.a.	7.3
1985[d]	12.1	9.6	2.2	n.a.	n.a.	n.a.	6.8
1986[d]	11.0	9.7	2.0	n.a.	n.a.	n.a.	6.5

n.a. Not available.

a. Entries are based on estimates of the average duration of completed spells of unemployment, which were derived from data on the average duration of in-progress spells of unemployment reported in Robert W. Bednarzik, "Layoffs and Permanent Job Losses: Workers' Traits and Cyclical Patterns," *Monthly Labor Review*, vol. 106 (September 1983), p. 10.

b. Entries are derived from the following identity: share of the labor force unemployed = share (incidence) of the labor force entering in a year × number of unemployment spells per person (assumed to be 1.0 for permanent layoffs) × average duration of a completed unemployment spell in years. Thus this column = 52 × column 3 ÷ column 1.

c. Data are from Bureau of Labor Statistics, *Employment and Earnings*, vols. 15–31 (January issues, 1969–84).

d. Forecasts for the first three columns are from regressions of permanent layoff unemployment duration, annual unemployment incidence, and unemployment share on current and lagged values of the civilian unemployment rate, all in log form, and from a linear time trend. Assumed civilian unemployment rates for years 1984, 1985, and 1986 are 7.3, 6.8, and 6.5 percent, respectively. These rates are 0.5 percentage point lower than comparable Congressional Budget Office estimates.

force experienced some unemployment due to permanent layoffs as opposed to 6.8 percent in 1979.[10]

Currently the United States is experiencing a rapid economic

10. Estimates of the annual incidence of unemployment caused by permanent layoffs may be slightly overstated; a small number of people experience more than one period of unemployment in a year.

recovery that may drive the unemployment rate down to 6.5 percent by 1986. The part of the unemployment rate caused by permanent layoffs is expected to fall to 2.0 percent, half the 1983 rate, and the proportion of workers who experience permanent layoffs should fall to 9.7 percent. Although these changes represent a substantial decrease, about 11 million workers will be permanently laid off and unemployed at some time during 1986.

Long-Term Unemployment

For workers permanently laid off, periods of unemployment averaged from ten to twenty weeks during the last decade (see table 6-3). Most periods of unemployment tend to be quite short,[11] but long periods, although relatively infrequent, account for a disproportionately large share of total unemployment. In 1978, for example, the long-term unemployed, those who were jobless for more than twenty-six weeks, represented 15 percent of the unemployed population, but they accounted for 40 percent of total weeks of unemployment.[12] In 1978 those unemployed more than twenty-six weeks because of permanent layoffs accounted for 0.3 percent of the labor force (see table 6-4). The 1982 recession quadrupled this rate. But as the economy recovers, the share of the labor force on permanent layoff should fall to about 2 percent by 1986, and the share of the labor force experiencing long-term unemployment because of permanent layoffs should decline to about 0.4 percent, equal to the rate attained in 1980.

If for simplicity we define a dislocated worker as one who experiences more than twenty-six weeks of unemployment because of a permanent layoff, we can estimate that in 1986 the economy will dislocate workers at an annual rate of 0.2 to

11. Kim B. Clark and Lawrence H. Summers, "Labor Market Dynamics and Unemployment: A Reconsideration," *BPEA, 1:1979*, pp. 13–72; and George A. Akerlof and Brian G. M. Main, "Unemployment Spells and Unemployment Experience," *The American Economic Review*, vol. 70 (December 1980), pp. 885–93.

12. Norman Bowers, "Probing the Issues of Unemployment Duration," *Monthly Labor Review*, vol. 103 (July 1980), p. 30.

Table 6-4. *Percentage of the Labor Force Unemployed because of Permanent Separations, by Duration of In-Progress Periods of Unemployment, 1978–83*

| Year | Duration of in-progress unemployment spells | | | | All permanent separations |
	Less than 5 weeks	5 to 14 weeks	15 to 26 weeks	27+ weeks	
1978	0.6	0.6	0.3	0.3	1.8
1979	0.6	0.6	0.3	0.2	1.7
1980	0.7	0.8	0.4	0.4	2.3
1981	0.8	0.8	0.5	0.5	2.6
1982	1.5	1.2	0.6	0.5	3.8
1983	0.9	1.0	0.8	1.3	4.0

Source: Bureau of Labor Statistics, *Employment and Earnings*, vols. 26–31 (January issues, 1979–84).

0.3 percent, about 250,000 to 350,000 workers each year.[13] A third of a million people laid off and unable to find work for more than six months is a very serious problem, but it is a tiny fraction of the labor force—or even of the number of workers who experience some unemployment because of permanent layoffs—and hence would seem to be a problem that could be alleviated by well-constructed public policy.

Identifying Dislocated Workers

The financial costs of permanent layoffs are dominated initially by the loss of earnings, although unemployment insurance generally replaces up to 70 percent of these losses. Subsequent losses stem from the decline in earnings potential: one study of victims of plant closings found that reemployment earnings were initially 25 percent lower than those before

13. For this illustrative calculation, we ignore dislocated workers who experience large wage losses but remain unemployed for less than six months. There is evidence that this group may be small. See Robert L. Crosslin, James S. Hanna, and David W. Stevens, "Identification of Dislocated Workers Utilizing Unemployment Insurance Data: Results of a Five State Analysis," paper prepared for the National Commission for Employment Policy and the U.S. Department of Labor, Washington, D.C., April 1984.

The annual rate of dislocation is exactly equal to the unemployment rate for dislocated workers (predicted to be 0.4 percent) divided by the average duration of a completed period of unemployment for a dislocated worker. We have assumed that this average unemployment duration is between eighteen and twenty-four months.

layoff. Three to four years later, however, average earnings losses had declined to less than 5 percent.[14]

All the studies we have reviewed indicate that age, job tenure, and local labor market conditions affect the financial costs of permanent layoffs. However, the link between individual characteristics and financial distress is too weak to be of use in identifying at the time of layoff those workers who will ultimately suffer large costs from job loss. Because dislocated workers cannot be pre-identified on the basis of objective criteria, programs to assist them will need to be integrated with other programs to assist unemployed workers. For instance, labor market programs could be sequenced to provide progressively greater job assistance to individuals as their period of unemployment grows longer, although benefits for the long-term unemployed should not be so attractive that they provide significant disincentives for reemployment. Sequencing job assistance implies that at least minimal labor market assistance should be offered to all workers who are laid off, not just to workers who ultimately experience long-term unemployment.

Policies for Adjusting to Change

In the last several years business and labor leaders, politicians, analysts, and writers have become advocates of "industrial policy," a phrase with many meanings. To some it means simply that the United States should put more effort and resources into general policies to promote growth, innovation, and labor market adjustment. Such policies might include subsidies or tax incentives designed to encourage savings and investment, research and development, or retraining and relocation of dislocated workers. To others the phrase suggests greater government involvement in planning and carrying out

14. Arlene Holen, Christopher Jehn, and Robert P. Trost, "Earnings Losses of Workers Displaced by Plant Closings," CRC 423 (Alexandria, Va.: Public Research Institute, December 1981), pp. 19, 21. For summaries of the early research on this topic see Arlene Holen, "Losses to Workers Displaced by Plant Closure or Layoff: A Survey of the Literature" (Alexandria, Va.: Public Research Institute, July 1976); and Jeanne Prial Gordus, Paul Jarley, and Louis A. Ferman, *Plant Closings and Economic Dislocation* (Kalamazoo, Mich.: W.E. Upjohn Institute for Employment Research, 1981).

strategies for industrial change. They envision a government agency (or perhaps a tripartite body representing business, labor, and government) that would design a new industrial structure and allocate capital and other forms of assistance to industries and companies picked for special treatment (and special obligations) because they have potential for future growth or because they need rescue and revitalization.

These divergent industrial policy prescriptions reflect differences in diagnoses of the problem and in opinions as to what role is possible and desirable for the government. Those who advocate government allocation of resources to companies picked for special treatment typically believe that the United States must deal with a decline of manufacturing, especially smokestack industries, and its inability to compete in world markets, a decline that will not be alleviated by changes in fiscal and monetary policy. They also believe that government is more capable than the private market of identifying worthy recipients in advance and allocating resources to them effectively. We do not share either of these opinions.

As we stated earlier, much of the so-called structural problem in manufacturing results instead from macroeconomic conditions—weak demand and the high value of the dollar in foreign exchange markets—and requires macroeconomic solutions. Reducing the federal deficit and lowering interest rates would be good for economic growth generally and would especially benefit industries that compete in world markets. Structural policies designed to affect the composition of manufacturing output rather than its level are not appropriate to the solution of a primarily macroeconomic problem.

Even if we believed that structural problems were the prime cause of declining industries, we would still be skeptical of the ability of a government agency to identify potential growth industries more effectively than the market and to allocate resources on strictly economic criteria. The history of government efforts to allocate resources among industries, companies, cities, and depressed areas shows that such decisions generally reflect the political and lobbying strength of the entities and areas involved. A government agency that allocated industrial capital in response to constituent pressure could retard rather than facilitate structural change in the American economy.

Policy Criteria

High priority should be given to policies that foster economic growth. But sustained growth requires change, the transfer of people and resources from less productive to more productive uses as demand changes and technology advances. Moving people and resources is easier if the rest of the economy is growing, but even then change is frequently costly and painful for people, companies, and communities. It is always tempting to avoid the pain by retarding change—for example, by protecting an inefficient industry with tariffs, quotas, or other trade barriers. But such protection injures domestic consumers and lowers the general standard of living; it protects the few at the expense of the many, and the costs to the many are often not as visible as the benefits to the few.

We believe the following general principles should govern U.S. policy on adjustment to structural change:

—Policy should be as obvious or transparent as possible so that both the costs and the benefits are clearly visible.

—The United States should not only avoid protectionism itself but should ensure that other countries lower trade barriers and refrain from obstructing structural change in their own economies.

—Assistance to the victims of change should be direct, not indirect, and should facilitate rather than impede adjustment.

—Policy should promote general economic growth, not just with appropriate fiscal and monetary instruments, but also by means of more specific measures such as incentives for supporting research and development. The sections that follow discuss some more specific approaches to implementing these four principles.

Improving Information

The debate over whether the United States should have an industrial policy frequently sounds as though no policy now exists. In fact the United States already has an industrial policy— or rather many complex and conflicting industrial policies— but no way of assessing what its policy is. Legislation, implementation, and regulation happen incrementally, and the impact of new actions and their interplay with existing programs is very difficult to evaluate. Thus tax and antitrust laws, trade policies, defense expenditures, price supports, and regulations affect specific industries and industry in general in unknown ways. The aims and goals of one program may be diametrically opposed by another. If programs are to be made more consistent and effective, it must be determined what current policies exist and what their costs and effects are.

A first step would be to create a new government agency, possibly patterned after the Industries Assistance Commission (IAC) in Australia. The sole purpose of the agency would be to measure the consequences of government actions for specific industries and to publicize the findings. The agency could respond to requests for information from both the Congress and the administration and could also estimate the consequences of proposed policies that were referred to it. The methodology for making such estimates has been improved by the IAC, and further gains can be anticipated. The investment in knowledge would cost little and could pay handsome dividends in improved policy. Such an agency would have further benefits if it encouraged other countries to undertake similar efforts to make their policies more transparent to themselves as well as to us. The United States could require its agency to evaluate the policies of other countries, but other countries might prefer to do the job themselves. If information on all major trading countries were generally available, one could foresee an international negotiation that would be multilateral and truly reciprocal in reducing industrial distortions for the mutual benefit of everyone.

Trade Policy

For the last half century the United States has been a leader in the effort to reduce barriers to international trade, a movement that has greatly benefited itself and its trading partners. The depressed state of the world economy has led to a resurgence of protectionism, however, and pressure for trade protection has been especially heavy in the United States recently as recession and the unfavorable exchange rate combined to injure American industry. The Reagan administration has resisted this pressure, but has been forced to make frequent exceptions, many of whose costs are hidden. A recent disturbing trend in trade policy, for example, has been to use quotas or similar devices to provide protection where previously tariffs were used. Textiles and clothing, automobiles, and steel are all large product groups in which quotas exist. However, the restrictiveness of quotas and their costs to American consumers increase when the competitiveness of the American industry declines—exactly the wrong incentive for becoming efficient. Furthermore, quotas create windfalls that can be divided in strange ways. For example, the so-called voluntary quota by Japanese automobile producers on their exports to the United States forces American consumers to pay a windfall that goes mostly to Japanese automobile producers and their U.S. dealers and to a lesser extent to American autoworkers and firms producing cars in the United States. At the same time, quotas on steel and textiles may force the textile- and steel-using American automobile industry to pay extra for its materials, thus raising its costs.

The first step toward a more transparent trade policy would be to convert all quotas into equivalent tariffs. Tariffs would be more visible to consumers and would highlight the net consequences for producers of different products. And most important, rather than providing a windfall for foreign competition, the payment would go to the American government, helping to reduce the budget deficit. A second step would be to negotiate reductions in the tariffs.

The United States has assisted its industries for a variety of reasons—the interests of national security have prompted the highest expenditures—but rarely to help them become internationally competitive. Other governments do this regularly, however. How should the United States respond?

While some suggestions, such as matching other countries' subsidies and industrial aids, can be dismissed as unnecessary, administratively and legislatively chaotic, socially wasteful, and terribly expensive, some reasoned response may well be justified. Clearly one principle should be incorporated in any response: only those things that benefit the United States should be done, and measures should not be taken simply because they hurt challengers more than the United States.

In some cases government can help industry in its efforts to meet the foreign challenge by removing restrictions. Antitrust-based limitations on combining the R&D or marketing efforts of different companies, which made sense when there was no serious competition from foreign companies, are no longer desirable and should be explicitly removed. However, antitrust and trade policies interact. The world, not just the United States, is the appropriate area for judging market dominance, but not if restrictive trade policies limit foreign competition. The government should take the initiative in offering antitrust exemptions because the very act of discussing joint efforts among competing firms might be construed as being illegal. Similarly, the United States unilaterally imposes export limitations on its industries to control foreign corrupt practices and to protect national security. These limitations should be lifted unless an international agreement can be reached to ensure that foreign competitors abide by similar restrictions. The best response to a competitive challenge from abroad will come from within the industry, and the government should not stand in its way.

There may be reasons for the government to go further. It is widely believed that high-technology industries have dynamic economies of scale, that is, the more units the industries produce, the greater the knowledge and skill they acquire and the lower their cost of production. In other countries this argument is used to justify government funds to cover early losses because private capital markets are unlikely to accept the risks.

Should the United States respond in some way if other countries promote their own industries? The answer depends on exactly what other countries do and what instruments they use. If a government were merely to provide general support, say through a research grant or an interest subsidy for investment in physical plant, the United States need not respond. If the American industry is ahead, it should remain ahead as long as further progress can be made. Forcing American companies to glance over their shoulder at potential competitors keeps their attention focused on further productivity gains.

However, if another government were to use trade-distorting measures such as import restraints or export subsidies to promote its industry, a case could be made for a U.S. government response. These measures close off potential markets for American industry in the country using them, in third markets, and even in the United States and are thus very serious because they keep American companies from achieving economies of scale. While the existing countervailing duty law, which offsets such government subsidies, would apply when the foreigner uses these subsidies for export to the United States, the penalties are too small and uncertain to deter the practice, and the remedy does not apply to the loss of third markets, although the United States might encourage other countries to countervail.

It is argued with some justification that a few countries have helped create new industries behind trade barriers, and the industries then burst upon world markets fully competitive and at world scale. The practice of developing industries behind protective trade barriers with government subsidies should not be tolerated. The U.S. government should respond to this challenge, but several criteria need to be present to justify special countering actions. First, the industry (or product) must be specifically identified for government assistance in an industrial development plan (or "vision") in a developed country. Second, the country must be promoting the industry behind significant trade restraints. Third, the product or industry must be involved in high technology promising significant dynamic economies of scale. Thus efforts by developing countries to get a foothold in an established industry would not be included; indeed, economic theory has long recognized the infant-industry argument as a legitimate exception to free trade. However, developed countries such as Japan are not infants, and they cannot justify trade-distorting measures even for a new industry. Fourth, actual countering actions would be required only if the efforts of the foreign government were successful—and most of them fail. But because failure cannot be guaranteed at the start, a two-part U.S. procedure should be instituted: a qualification test and an implementation test (only when success is seen). Finally, the action must directly affect U.S. industry. If one advanced country attempted to catch up with another one (neither being the United States), there would be no grounds for keeping American consumers from enjoying underpriced imports.

How should the United States respond? When a country uses trade-distorting measures, existing remedies such as those under U.S. antidumping and countervailing duty statutes should be utilized in addition to any rights created by previous General Agreement on Tariffs and Trade negotiations. However, to have any deterrent value, more serious actions are called for. The United States should make strong representation to the offending country to remove its trade restraints in view of its promotional program. A possible response would be to introduce into U.S. laws a mechanism to help the American industry gain access by imposing a penalty tariff of, say, 100 percent against the products of the offending country if it should refuse to permit free entry. Furthermore, the United States might want to match subsidies to protect third markets, but on a very selective basis. Tactics might require such a capability even if it were never used. A strong deterrent to unfair trade practices, if effective, would be invoked only rarely.

The United States would have to recognize the responsibility that comes with devising such a countering strategy. The government would need a fail-safe system that could not be used for protectionist purposes. It would constantly have to bring the countering strategy to the attention of other industrial countries for it to have its full deterrent effect. Finally, the policy must be fully reciprocal. The United States must accept foreign competition in its market, even for the most sensitive high-technology goods.

Helping Dislocated Workers

In addition to revamping trade policies, an important way to facilitate structural change is to help dislocated workers find new jobs in which they can apply their skills and experience. Fortunately, if the economy continues to grow and unemployment continues to decline, the number of workers laid off and unable to find work for as long as six months is likely to be less than 0.5 percent of the labor force. But the difficulty in designing policy is that there is no accurate way to predict which workers are going to have the most trouble finding jobs and to focus attention on them.

Job turnover in the United States is high. At 6.5 percent unemployment about 23 million people, or 20 percent of the labor force, will experience some unemployment during a year because they are laid off, quit their job, or are just entering or reentering the labor force. The economy will function better if all of these people, not just dislocated workers, can be matched to appropriate jobs relatively quickly and easily. Hence, the United States may need a sequence of job assistance efforts: (1) a general effort to improve job information and to match job openings with job seekers at relatively low cost per placement and (2) a more intensive and costly attempt to place and if necessary retrain those who turn out to need the most help.

Job Search and Relocation. The nature of job searching differs widely among individuals with different levels of formal education and occupational specialization. Inexperienced workers with at least a minimum competence in basic skills tend to find jobs rather quickly. In fact, entrants and reentrants to the labor force typically try out several jobs before they find a match that is mutually acceptable to both worker and employer. However, experienced workers with more specialized skills have fewer job openings to choose from. Although they are less likely to quit or lose their jobs, when they do become unemployed they are forced to sift through a large number of job openings in order to find one that requires their skills.

A worker with highly transferable skills is more immune to declines in occupational demand and has access to a wider menu of job openings than other experienced workers. Individuals with extensive formal education (for example, college training) find jobs more quickly than other experienced workers, while well-paid workers with highly specialized training but limited formal schooling (for example, less than a high school education) tend to fare the poorest in the labor market.[15] This suggests that there might be an advantage to providing

15. Terry R. Johnson, Katherine P. Dickinson, and Richard W. West, "Older Workers' Responses to Job Displacement and the Assistance Provided by the Employment Service," National Commission for Employment Policy Research Report 83-13 (Washington, D.C.: NCEP, 1983).

basic education to older, poorly educated workers in declining industries while they are still employed.

For experienced workers, searching for a job can be complicated by the fact that the demand for particular skills may be weak either locally or at the national level. Even if appropriate jobs are available in a distant labor market, relocation costs are often high for older workers because they are likely to own their own homes, have a working spouse, and have strong ties to family and community. Hence it is not surprising that over a five-year period people between the ages of twenty-five and twenty-nine are three times as likely to have moved from one county or one state to another as are people between the ages of fifty-five and sixty-four.[16] The combination of job shortages for some experienced workers, the thinness of the market for their specialized skills, and their greater reluctance to relocate contribute to longer periods of unemployment.

How do workers find jobs? Surveys indicate they most often use informal methods of job seeking, directly contacting employers, asking friends and relatives about job openings, or responding to newspaper ads. Only a small proportion—about 11 percent, according to the survey reported in table 6-5—find jobs through either state or private employment agencies.

Although the American labor exchange may work well for most workers most of the time, its informal, personal character makes it inadequate to the needs of dislocated workers, especially older workers with specialized skills. Senior workers who have not searched for a job in many years may have weak job-search skills and be unaware of current employment opportunities. Moreover, the shutdown of a large plant or a reduction in force that results in the layoff of friends and relatives may dry up a worker's job information. Such a result may be particularly acute in relatively small labor markets. Local employment services are unlikely to be able to meet the sudden rise in the demand for job placements following a major plant closing. Finally, informal job networks seem especially ill equipped to provide information about distant job opportuni-

16. Bureau of the Census, *Current Population Reports*, series P-20, no. 368, "Geographic Mobility: March 1975 to March 1980" (GPO, 1981), p. 19.

Table 6-5. *Job-Seeking and Job-Finding Methods*
Percent of unemployed workers surveyed in 1972[a]

Method	Used method to look for work	Method by which current job was obtained
Applied directly to employer	66.0	34.9
Asked friends		
About jobs where they work	50.8	12.4
About jobs elsewhere	41.8	5.5
Asked relatives		
About jobs where they work	28.4	6.1
About jobs elsewhere	27.3	2.2
Answered newspaper ads		
Local	45.9	12.2
Nonlocal	11.7	1.3
Private employment agency	21.0	5.6
State employment agency	33.5	5.1
School placement or teacher referral	22.9	4.4
Civil service test	15.3	2.1
Union hiring hall	6.0	1.5
Other	n.a.	6.7

Source: Bureau of Labor Statistics, *Job Seeking Methods Used by American Workers*, Bulletin 1886 (GPO, 1975), pp. 4, 7. The average number of methods used to look for work was 4.0.

n.a. Not available.

a. The approximately 3.5 million persons surveyed do not represent the total number of unemployed workers in 1972.

ties. These factors suggest that having a formal state or nationwide apparatus to assist the job search of dislocated workers may be especially useful.

Training. While experienced workers may find little market for their particular job skills, in other respects they possess characteristics that are prized by employers: job commitment, discipline, and productive work habits. An obvious route to increasing the employability of dislocated workers is retraining. In fact, most laid-off workers receive substantial retraining, although much of this is on the job rather than in a formal setting before reemployment. Most job skills, in fact, are better taught on the job than in classrooms.

There is an important role for formal training and retraining to assist dislocated workers, however. Case studies of crash retraining programs suggest that students with prior exposure to training material, related job training, or a strong background in fundamental skills such as mathematics are much more likely than other students to master the curriculum and obtain a job using their acquired skills.[17] There could be advantages in providing training to these workers well in advance of their permanent layoffs, particularly in those industries subject to the highest risk of job loss. For example, the United Auto Workers–General Motors and UAW-Ford training funds provide both employed and laid-off auto workers with tuition assistance for training at local colleges and technical institutes, retraining in high-growth occupations, and career counseling. They are financed by employer contributions equal to $0.05 per hour for each hour worked by employees.

Retraining dislocated workers in three- to twelve-month courses appears to be most successful when it attempts to build on their existing skills and natural aptitudes. Not all unemployed workers should become computer programmers, especially those without appropriate previous work or educational experience. Moreover, experienced workers who have been away from the classroom for years may have difficulty learning in a formal setting. Finally, studies of the earnings effects of education indicate that a year of training is associated with an increase in earnings of approximately 10 percent. Thus, even in the best of circumstances, six months of traditional training would fail to eliminate wage losses of 30 to 40 percent.

Existing Programs to Assist Workers. Permanently laid-off workers are currently served by three federal programs: the U.S. Employment Service, which provides job search assistance; the Job Training Partnership Act (JTPA), which supports job-search and relocation assistance, training, and other activities; and unemployment insurance, which compensates workers for the loss of earnings caused by joblessness. In addition, there are a number of federal programs (for example, trade adjustment assistance) that provide income assistance to specific groups of unemployed workers but little in the way of adjustment services.

The U.S. Employment Service consists of over 2,000 offices throughout the country funded by the federal government and

---

17. See, for instance, Jay Mathews, "Retraining '83: The Class in Room E221," *Washington Post*, November 6–9, 1983; and Gordus, Jarley, and Ferman, *Plant Closings and Economic Dislocation*, p. 108.

subject to procedures and guidelines established by the Department of Labor but operated by the states. Studies of the Employment Service have found that it does a very poor job of assisting experienced workers who are unemployed. It has the reputation of catering to economically disadvantaged job seekers with poor job skills and in fact has very few listings for well-paying jobs.[18] By contrast, Sweden requires that all job vacancies be listed with the public labor exchange.[19] The effectiveness of the Employment Service has been sharply limited because it is not primarily in the business of job counseling and job placement. The Employment Service administers work tests for unemployment insurance and other programs, for instance; and despite a growing number of federally and state mandated responsibilities and a large increase in the labor force, the number of its employees has remained approximately constant from 1966 to 1981.

In late 1982 Congress enacted the Job Training Partnership Act, under which title III authorized a modest program to assist dislocated workers. The dislocated-worker program began during the fall of 1983, with expected annual expenditures of $223 million in federal money and about $180 million in matching state expenditures. Although federally financed, title III activities are the responsibility of the governor of each state. In most cases this is a new state responsibility, and it will be some time before each develops a capacity to design and deliver services.

Title III permits a wide range of activities to assist dislocated workers, including job-search assistance, job development, training, counseling, assistance before layoff, commuting and relocation aid, and early assistance in the event of plant closings. Funding for wages, allowances, and stipends, however, is severely limited. Participation is open to workers subject to permanent layoffs who are eligible for or have exhausted

18. Terry R. Johnson and others, "A National Evaluation of the Impact of the United States Employment Service," paper prepared for the Department of Labor, August 1982.

19. Marc Bendick, Jr., "The Swedish 'Active Labor Market' Approach to Reemploying Workers Dislocated by Economic Change," *Journal of Health and Human Resources Administration*, vol. 6 (Fall 1983), pp. 209–24.

unemployment insurance and are unlikely to return to their previous industry or occupation, workers unemployed because of plant closings, and the long-term unemployed. These criteria are loose enough to permit states to assist most unemployed workers. It is still too early to evaluate the performance of the program because most of the key programmatic choices—the administrative structure of the program, the type of assistance, and the selection of program participants—are still being made by the states.

Unemployment insurance is available during the period of the job search to most workers who are unemployed because of permanent layoffs. Most states provide recipients of unemployment insurance with up to twenty-six weeks of benefits equal to 70 percent of their previous earnings. The federal government generally provides extended benefits during recessions.

Although unemployment insurance provides valuable support to workers while they are unemployed, the program does not incorporate a strong incentive for individuals to return to work. Additionally, some states have been reluctant to allow recipients to participate full time in retraining programs. Total unemployment insurance expenditures amounted to $29 billion in fiscal year 1983 and are expected to decline to $16 billion in fiscal year 1985.

Improving the Labor Market. The following proposals are based on the premise that adjustment to structural change in the economy would be facilitated both by improving the functioning of the labor market generally—so that job seekers are more quickly and easily matched to appropriate job openings—and by more intensive efforts to provide assistance to experienced workers who have lost their jobs.

First, the U.S. government should modernize the Employment Service so that experienced workers can obtain rapid access to information on job opportunities matched to their talents and interests. This would require a significant expansion in the volume of job listings it handles. A first step would be to enforce an existing federal requirement that all federal contractors list their job openings with the Employment Service. Ultimately, it should be possible for employers and workers to rapidly retrieve information on job applicants and job openings in local and distant labor markets.[20]

Second, the federal government should provide all unemployed workers access to a limited battery of job search services soon after they receive notification of an impending layoff or after they become unemployed. These services could include help in writing a resumé, training in interview techniques, assessing the strength of the labor market in the fields for which they are qualified, counseling on opportunities for retraining and geographic relocation, developing a job search strategy, providing access to the job placement and job matching services of the Employment Service office, and screening for participation in more extensive help targeted to dislocated workers. These services could be provided by expanded and reorganized Employment Service offices. Many unemployed workers would neither need nor choose to make extensive use of them. However, early contact between unemployed workers and an efficient labor exchange would allow workers with serious reemployment problems to begin receiving assistance at the earliest possible stage.[21]

Third, the government needs to provide additional assistance to workers with extended unemployment or those identified in the first stage as needing greater assistance. Inexperienced workers who would benefit from additional schooling or training could be referred to community colleges and technical institutes or to the employment and training program funded by title II of the Job Training Partnership Act. Experienced workers would have access to training options that are described below. For most unemployed workers, the second stage would emphasize intensive job-search assistance and counseling. The

20. It would also be desirable to alter the organizational structure of the Employment Service. Currently it is a joint federal and state program. Legislation in 1982 also created a formal link between it and the Private Industry Councils that oversee the Job Training Partnership Act. It appears that the performance of the Employment Service has suffered from the lack of accountability to a single authority. Alternative organizational structures include fully federalizing the Employment Service system, turning it over to the states, or setting it up as a nonprofit institution along the lines of the postal service.

21. For a related proposal to provide assistance to dislocated workers soon after they become unemployed, see Malcom R. Lovell, Jr., "The Displaced Worker: A New Approach to Encourage Reemployment" (unpublished paper, Brookings Institution, October 1983).

job counseling would be designed to help them develop a realistic appraisal of their labor market opportunities and learn strategies for finding, rejecting, and accepting job offers. Tests to measure aptitude and vocational interest could also be made available to workers contemplating career changes.

Assistance could also be provided through job clubs, which consist of groups of no more than twenty-five individuals who meet regularly to receive training and to practice techniques in job search and self-presentation. Job listings, telephones, and other materials are provided. A notable feature of job clubs is that participants appear to interact in a supportive manner, often exchanging information on job openings and generating an atmosphere of peer pressure and moral support that stimulates search efforts.[22]

Fourth, the federal government should provide emergency teams to assist in local labor markets that experience closings of large plants or major reductions in force. Labor market institutions are apt to be overwhelmed by sudden increases in unemployment. For example, in many areas Employment Service personnel are diverted from job placement activities during a surge in unemployment so that unemployment insurance claims can be processed. In Canada the Manpower Consultative Service is available to assist localities that experience plant closings or mass layoffs.[23]

Since 1980 the California Economic Adjustment Team has worked with communities, businesses, and labor organizations affected by plant closings to find new jobs for displaced workers. The federal government also has experience in this area through the Defense Department's Economic Adjustment Program, which has assisted a number of areas affected by base closings since the early 1960s.[24]

Fifth, workers need to be encouraged to participate in training

22. Marc Bendick, Jr., "The Role of Public Programs and Private Markets in Reemploying Displaced Workers," *Policy Studies Review*, vol. 2 (May 1983), pp. 729–30.

23. See Michael C. Barth and Fritzie Reisner, "Work Adjustment to Plant Shutdowns and Mass Layoffs: An Analysis of Program Experience and Policy Options," paper prepared for the National Alliance of Business (Washington, D.C.: ICF, August 1981); and William L. Batt, Jr., "Canada's Good Example with Displaced Workers," *Harvard Business Review*, vol. 83 (July–August 1983), pp. 6–22.

24. Charles R. Frank, Jr., *Foreign Trade and Domestic Aid* (Brookings Institution, 1977), pp. 72–79.

and education programs while they are still employed. Spread over a number of years, prelayoff training could potentially increase the mobility of the work force and reduce the costs of job dislocation. There is evidence that such training ultimately raises the value of further training after a layoff. While investment in formal worker training has tended to end at age twenty-five or thirty, an emphasis on lifelong learning may be more suited to a technologically progressive society. Moreover, many older workers were not a part of the expansion in educational attainment levels that occurred in the 1960s and, if laid off, face the risk of large reductions in earning capacity.

Specifically, the government could encourage firms to adopt training programs similar to the UAW–Ford–General Motors programs, which now receive some JTPA funding in addition to the employer contributions. A federal subsidy for such training funds could be provided with the requirement that the firms contribute at some matching rate, say $2 for every $1 of federal funds.

Finally, experienced workers certified as dislocated should be permitted to participate in full-time training without forfeiting eligibility for unemployment insurance. In 1976 Congress passed legislation that required states to allow unemployment insurance recipients to participate in state-approved training programs, but unfortunately many states have allowed only limited numbers of them to pursue this option.[25] Funds for retraining programs could come from a mixture of sources, including worker contributions from savings, loans financed by the federal student aid program, and direct federal expenditures. Requiring that workers contribute some of their own funds to pay for retraining might screen out those who are not seriously interested in training. Eligibility for unemployment insurance benefits while in training would also have to be contingent on attaining minimal levels of academic achievement. Careful efforts to limit abuses of federal funding of training and of unemployment insurance income are important because both are relatively expensive.

25. Richard Corrigan and Rochelle L. Stanfield, "Casualties of Change," *National Journal*, vol. 16 (February 11, 1984), pp. 261–62.

Beyond these recommendations we would urge that some consideration be given to compensating the most severely affected victims of structural change. Society could provide financial compensation to all or selected classes of workers (for instance, older workers permanently laid off) as it did under the trade adjustment assistance program. A wage insurance scheme in which the level of compensation varies directly with the level of wage loss would eliminate much of the work disincentive associated with unemployment insurance and thereby reduce its program expenditures. Such a program might include a deductible of 5 percent of previous hourly wages and a coinsurance rate of 25 percent. In other words, after a wage decline of 5 percent, the program would reimburse a worker for 75 percent of any additional decline. A worker whose wages fell from $12 an hour to $8 an hour (a 33 percent decline) would receive an insurance payment of $2.55 an hour, raising the net wage to $10.55 an hour (representing a 12 percent decline). A worker who experienced a 50 percent pay cut would find that his insured wage declined by only 16 percent. The scheme provides a strong work incentive because compensation is paid in proportion to the number of hours worked. Total program costs could be controlled by varying the length of the program and the coinsurance and deductibility provisions.[26] To further limit costs, it would probably be desirable to restrict participation in the program to older, more experienced workers who have lost their jobs because of an identifiable structural change.

Funding Adjustment Programs. Although we have not made precise estimates of the cost of each policy option for facilitating adjustment to structural change, the total program could cost $2 billion. Initial costs could be lower if options are phased in gradually. Given legitimate concerns about the size of the deficit, additional expenditures should be financed by an increase in taxes or cuts in spending elsewhere. The economy as a whole would benefit if costly and inefficient restraints on international competition—including quotas in the steel and

26. Administering the program would require collecting information on past and current hourly wages and hours worked. These data are not currently collected by the unemployment insurance system.

auto industries—were phased out in favor of a policy of facilitating adjustment to structural change.

Support for Research and Development

A final set of policies designed to increase general economic growth involves government encouragement of research and development. There are strong reasons to believe that R&D is essential to sustained economic growth and that private markets tend to underfund R&D. But government funding should be undertaken with great caution because political processes may not lead to the best choices among potential projects. In this brief section we explore the case for government encouragement of industrial R&D and suggest some general principles for government involvement in basic research and commercial development.

Why R&D May Be Underfunded. A company investing in R&D expects that research will increase profits, that it will yield information leading to new and better products or to lower production costs. But the information resulting from R&D often becomes available to competitors who copy the new products or processes without having incurred the costs of the R&D. Because the innovating company cannot keep the information to itself, its rate of return may be much less than the return to society as a whole through, for instance, widespread dissemination of a new product. Companies are thus likely to invest less in R&D than would be desirable from the point of view of the whole economy.

Studies of various industries have found that the rate of return to society is typically two or more times as high as the rate of return to a company for research activities it has conducted. Moreover, these estimated annual returns to society on the investment are typically in the vicinity of 30 to 50 percent and are even higher in the agricultural sector.[27] These high rates are convincing evidence that private industry un-

27. See Edwin Mansfield and others, *Technology Transfer, Productivity, and Economic Policy* (W.W. Norton, 1982), pp. 183–91; and Robert E. Evenson, Paul E. Waggoner, and Vernon W. Ruttan, "Economic Benefits from Research: An Example from Agriculture," *Science*, vol. 205 (September 14, 1979), pp. 1101–07.

derfunds R&D and that public subsidies might have a high payoff.

In addition, even if the results of R&D could be appropriated solely by the innovating company, investment in major product or process innovations may involve large expenditures, high risks, and long lead times. Capital markets may fail to provide funds for these kinds of investments, especially in industries characterized by many small- or medium-sized companies, even though the returns to the companies are likely to be high, typically in the range of 15 to 30 percent annually.

If federal policies to promote R&D were optimal, funds would flow into the most profitable opportunities and private and social rates of return on additional investment would be much lower. Thus, although the evidence cannot suggest an absolute level of optimal federal support, it does suggest that increasing the federal role would be of substantial social and private value.

Basic Research. The results of basic research are likely to be very general and to have applications that extend beyond a single firm or industry. Basic research is inherently risky and may not pay off for a long time, if at all. Nor can its results be easily protected with patents. Even allowing firms to spread the risk of basic research by engaging in joint ventures may not produce a desirable level of investigation whose results are available to form the basis of future innovations. Hence basic research is particularly likely to be underfunded by the market— or funded in inefficient, duplicative ways—and is a strong candidate for federal subsidy.

Federal subsidies for research have taken the forms of tax incentives and direct funding.[28] In the case of basic research the two policies are not equivalent because of the riskiness of the endeavor and the difficulty in defining research expenditures. Although special tax provisions are expected to generate additional R&D,[29] the shift to high-risk, long-lead-time ventures will be incremental. Moreover, it is difficult to design a tax incentive program that is not subject to substantial abuse. A

28. For a succinct overview of current R&D tax policy see Edwin Mansfield, "Tax Policy and Innovation," *Science*, vol. 215 (March 12, 1982), pp. 1365–71.
29. Ibid.

recent study of the R&D tax credit instituted as part of the Economic Recovery Tax Act of 1981, for instance, estimated that the loss of federal revenues from reduced taxes was three times the actual increase in R&D because companies reclassified other expenditures as research to qualify for special tax treatment.[30]

Commercial Development. Development efforts involve a separate set of concerns from basic research. Critics frequently cite lack of government expertise as a problem in development, where projects should be chosen because of commercial as well as technical potential. A recent study distinguishes successful projects (for instance, those in the Agricultural Research Service) as having structures that allow significant industrial participation in choosing the project. Unsuccessful efforts, on the other hand—those in the short-lived cooperative automotive research program, for instance—are often motivated primarily by government.[31] The precept that government cannot be expected to choose future "winning" industries for development purposes applies even more strongly to developing specific technical innovations within an industry.[32] Moreover, even if the government had the information on which to base decisions on what development projects to fund, it is not apparent that the best choice would result. Political motives can militate against high-risk development endeavors, the very projects for which efficiency considerations would recommend federal subsidies.[33]

An additional concern is that large-scale funding of a project automatically establishes a politically important pressure group with a stake in the status quo. The appeal of the project to the

30. Edwin Mansfield, "Public Policy toward Industrial Innovation: An International Study of R&D Tax Credits," paper presented at the 75th Anniversary Colloquium on Productivity and Technology of the Harvard Business School, 1984.

31. Richard R. Nelson, "Government Support of Technical Progress: Lessons from History," *Journal of Policy Analysis and Management*, vol. 2 (Summer 1983), pp. 499–514.

32. See, for example, Robert Lawrence, "The Questionable Case for Selective Industrial Policies," paper prepared for the meeting of the Southern Economic Association, November 1983; and Charles Schultze, "Industrial Policy: A Dissent," *The Brookings Review*, vol. 2 (Fall 1983), pp. 3–12.

33. Linda Cohen and Roger Noll, "Electoral Influences on Congressional Policy Preferences," paper prepared for the Stanford Conference on the Political Economy of Public Policy, March 1984.

group is based on project expenditures as well as—or perhaps instead of—project results. Consequently the appeal of the project for a legislator will be partly based on continued project expenditures, and the timing and nature of investments will be difficult to adjust to changes in economic conditions or unexpected resolution of technical problems.

This concern has several negative implications for direct federal oversight of a commercially oriented development project. Some projects that would have otherwise succeeded may fail because of inflexible management. Projects that should have been canceled may persist for years after they have proved commercially infeasible. Finally, the attempt to continue a big development project may divert resources from other R&D programs that lack the political support attendant on expensive "centerpiece" projects. Thus the now-defunct Clinch River Breeder Reactor demonstration, whose cost to the federal government was originally estimated at a modest 2 percent of the total that the government planned to spend on breeder reactor research, ultimately was projected to require at least 36 percent of total expenditures; and when the space shuttle project encountered unanticipated cost overruns, the National Aeronautics and Space Administration witnessed a steady erosion of space science funding.[34]

This discussion suggests some guidelines for R&D policy. First, direct subsidies are generally an effective way to encourage basic research. Joint ventures are unlikely to address the problem of adequate returns to innovative companies, and indirect subsidies are both unduly expensive and unlikely to generate the appropriate mix of products. Direct subsidies, however, are not recommended for large development efforts because political incentives are likely to generate poor project choices and project management and may undermine the overall R&D effort. Consequently, such structural strategies as encouraging joint ventures may be the appropriate role for government for promoting commercial development.

Trends in Federal R&D Funding. Table 6–6 shows federal

34. Linda Cohen and Roger Noll, "The Political Economy of Government Programs to Promote New Technology," paper prepared for the meeting of the American Political Science Association, September 1983.

Table 6-6. *Federal Research and Development Obligations, by Type of Activity, Fiscal Years 1973–84*[a]

Fiscal year	Total 1972 dollars[b] (thousands)	Percent change	Basic research 1972 dollars[b] (thousands)	Percent change	Applied research 1972 dollars[b] (thousands)	Percent change	Development 1972 dollars[b] (thousands)	Percent change
1973	8,685.2	. . .	1,853.0	. . .	2,136.7	. . .	4,091.0	. . .
1974	8,537.0	−2	1,856.5	0	2,365.2	11	3,783.5	−7
1975	8,647.7	1	1,852.9	0	2,437.6	3	3,828.0	−1
1976	9,035.4	4	1,865.9	1	2,791.5	15	3,847.9	1
1977	10,102.3	12	2,090.8	12	2,835.4	2	4,508.3	17
1978	10,792.1	7	2,232.3	7	3,051.3	8	4,786.8	6
1979	11,027.3	2	2,321.4	4	2,994.2	−2	4,959.8	4
1980	10,933.9	−1	2,373.1	2	2,986.1	0	4,801.2	−3
1981	10,265.2	−6	2,321.8	−2	2,708.0	−9	4,603.3	−4
1982[c]	9,550.8	−7	2,265.1	−2	2,479.3	−8	4,220.8	−8
1983[c]	9,080.5	−5	2,334.0	3	2,321.2	−6	3,988.4	−6
1984[c]	7,832.8	−14	2,665.2	14	2,478.4	7	2,165.9	−46

Sources: Data for fiscal years 1973–83 are from National Science Foundation, *Federal Funds for Research and Development: Fiscal Years 1981, 1982, and 1983*, vol. 31 (GPO, 1982), pp. 172, 176, 179, 181, and 183; data for fiscal year 1984 are from NSF, *Federal Funds for Research and Development: Fiscal Years 1982, 1983, and 1984*, vol. 32 (GPO, 1983), pp. 160, 164, 167, 169, and 171.

a. Department of Defense R&D expenditures are not included.

b. Fiscal year deflators are based on quarterly GNP deflators from Data Resources, Inc. Totals include expenditures for R&D plant.

c. Estimated. Actual figures for fiscal years 1982 and 1983 are not used because of changes in expenditure classifications.

budget obligations by type of R&D activity (excluding activities of the Department of Defense) for the past decade. Real expenditures have declined each year since 1979. Before 1984 the biggest decline occured in the applied research category, where real expenditures dropped by 22 percent from 1980 to 1983. The fiscal year 1984 funding levels show a marked shift in this pattern. Development funding declined dramatically, largely because the space shuttle development program was completed; its operational expenses are not included in the federal R&D budget. The large decline in total R&D expenditures is also the result of reclassifying shuttle expenditures. Basic and applied research funding increased substantially. However, combined funding for basic and applied research was 4 percent lower in 1984 than at its peak in 1980.

Our discussion has suggested that the research components instead of development should be emphasized in the R&D budget. While the 1984 decline in development obligations should be treated with caution because of this component's sensitivity to single projects, current funding priorities do reflect a move in the direction of research. Our discussion also has suggested that an increase in funding for basic research is appropriate. While current plans call for such an increase, the level of research funding is still below the fiscal 1980 total, reflecting a penny-wise approach to the use of federal resources.

7

Helping the Poor

AMERICANS live comfortably in comparison with the rest of the world and with earlier generations in their own country. But not everyone shares in the general affluence. In 1982 more than 34 million people—about 15 percent of the population—had incomes below the government's official poverty line. Between 1979 and 1982 the percentage of the population in poverty rose steadily to the level of the mid-1960s.

Moreover, the chances of being poor are not passed out randomly. In 1982, 12 percent of whites were poor, compared with 36 percent of blacks and 30 percent of Hispanics. Families headed by a woman were far more likely to be poor than other families. Indeed, for some groups, poverty was the norm rather than the exception. More than 70 percent of the children living in families headed by a black woman were poor.[1]

In previous chapters, we have urged that high priority be given to policies designed to keep the economy growing at a healthy rate. Growth not only raises the average standard of living; it also makes it easier to finance government services, find new opportunities for dislocated workers, and assist the poor.

But significant reductions in poverty will not be automatic even if growth is sustained. To be sure, some of the recent

Alice M. Rivlin undertook primary responsibility for drafting this chapter.

1. U.S. Bureau of the Census, *Current Population Reports*, series P-60, no. 144, "Characteristics of the Population Below the Poverty Level: 1982" (Government Printing Office, 1984), p. 8.

increase in poverty is related to the 1980–82 recession and will be reversed as the economic recovery proceeds. But poverty is now heavily concentrated in groups that are not likely to share automatically in the greater general prosperity, especially minorities and women with children.

A major challenge to public policy, then, is to find ways of ensuring that the fruits of economic growth can be more widely shared. The United States should not tolerate a permanent underclass that is shunted aside as the rest of the population improves its standard of living. This brief chapter serves to highlight the problem and to suggest some solutions.

Measuring Poverty

Since the 1960s, when the United States rediscovered the paradox of poverty in an affluent society, the government has kept a count of those whose incomes fall below an official poverty line.[2] The government's definition of poverty income is adjusted for type and size of family and for changes in the cost of living. Income is measured before taxes and includes cash transfer payments, such as social security and welfare, but not in-kind benefits, such as food stamps.

By this measure, over 22 percent of the total population lived in poverty in 1960 (see table 7-1). The incidence of poverty dropped quite rapidly in the 1960s and more slowly in the early 1970s. By 1974 only about 11 percent of the population lived below the official poverty line.

These quite dramatic reductions in poverty resulted from a combination of strong economic growth and increased transfer payments. Through most of this period real wages were rising and unemployment was declining. Social security benefits increased substantially, contributing to the reduction of poverty among the aged, and transfer payments aimed specifically at the poor grew.

Progress against poverty was interrupted by the 1975–76

2. That line was initially defined by taking what nutritionists in the Department of Agriculture determined to be the cost of an "economical" diet for a family of four and multiplying that figure by four, since in the early 1960s it was thought that roughly a quarter of a family's income was spent on food.

Table 7-1. *Percentage of the Population below the Poverty Level,*
1960–82

Year	Percent	Year	Percent
1960	22.2	1971	12.5
1961	21.9	1972	11.9
1962	21.0	1973	11.1
1963	19.5	1974	11.2
1964	19.0	1975	12.3
1965	17.3	1976	11.8
1966	14.7	1977	11.6
1967	14.2	1978	11.4
1968	12.8	1979	11.7
1969	12.1	1980	13.0
1970	12.6	1981	14.0
		1982	15.0

Sources: For 1960–64, U.S. Bureau of the Census, *Current Population Reports,* series P-60, no. 68, "Poverty in the United States: 1959 to 1968" (Government Printing Office, 1969), p. 24; for 1965–82, *Current Population Reports,* series P-60, no. 144, "Characteristics of the Population Below the Poverty Level: 1982" (GPO, 1984), p. 7.

recession and was slow for the rest of the decade. The proportion of households with cash incomes below the poverty line in 1979 was only half a percentage point lower than a decade earlier. The lack of improvement in the 1970s was related to slow economic growth, rising unemployment, and high inflation, although these negative factors were offset by continued increases in real cash transfers.

The decline in poverty was dramatically reversed after 1979: the poverty rate rose about 1 percentage point each year from 1979 through 1982. The rate in 1982, the last year for which complete figures are available, was the highest since 1965.

The 1980–82 recession was longer (though no deeper) than the recession of 1975–76, but it had a much more serious impact on poverty than did the earlier recession. Growth in the real value of cash transfers cushioned the impact of the 1975–76 recession. In the most recent recession, cuts in the real value of those benefits aggravated the effect of unfavorable economic conditions on the poor. A substantially higher fraction of the unemployed received unemployment insurance benefits in 1975–76 than in 1980–82.[3] While real increases in social security

3. Testimony of Gary Burtless before the Subcommittees on Oversight and on Public Assistance and Unemployment Compensation of the House Committee on Ways and Means, October 18, 1983.

benefits protected the aged from increases in poverty, the assistance relied on by many of the nonelderly poor was reduced in real terms. The average value of the public assistance (aid to families with dependent children and general assistance) received by a poor family rose 5 percent after inflation between 1974 and 1977; that value declined 17 percent between 1979 and 1982.

Since the distribution of income other than transfers appears to be increasingly unequal, even a period of sustained growth may not lead to reductions in poverty in the future unless the recent declines in the real value of means-tested cash transfers are reversed.[4]

The official poverty line is a crude measuring instrument and numerous efforts have been made to refine it. One set of refinements designed to provide a more accurate indication of changes in the well-being of the low-income population includes in-kind benefits in the definition of income used to determine poverty. Considering only cash incomes gives an incomplete picture of changes in poverty, since government aid to the poor in the form of food stamps, housing, and medical care benefits has increased substantially since the 1960s.[5]

It is not clear how noncash benefits should be valued, however, since their market value (the cost the government has to pay) may be greater than their value to the recipient (what he would actually have spent if given money rather than the in-kind benefit). Several alternative valuation methods have been suggested.

Not surprisingly, inclusion of in-kind benefits in income reduces the incidence of poverty no matter what valuation

4. One recent study finds that over 1967–79, rises in incomes reduced poverty 2.4 percentage points and changes in the shape of the income distribution increased poverty 2.9 percentage points; both of these effects were dominated by the 3.1-percentage-point reduction attributable to growth in real transfers. Over 1979–82, the comparable figures are 0.8, 2.9, and − 0.4 percentage points, respectively; the transfer effect was overwhelmed. See Peter Gottschalk and Sheldon Danziger, "Macroeconomic Conditions, Income Transfers, and the Trend in Poverty" (University of Wisconsin–Madison, Institute for Research on Poverty, September 1983), p. 21.

5. Cash benefits accounted for 76 percent of all means-tested assistance to the poor in 1965, while noncash benefits accounted for the remainder. By 1982, those proportions were nearly reversed: noncash benefits were 64 percent of means-tested assistance, while cash benefits amounted to only 36 percent of the total.

Table 7-2. *Percentage of the Population below the Poverty Level, Adjusted for In-Kind Transfers, Selected Years, 1965–82*

Year	Percent[a]
1965	12.1
1968	9.9
1970	9.3
1972	6.2
1974	7.2
1976	6.7
1979	6.1
1982	8.8[b]

Source: Timothy M. Smeeding, "The Anti-Poverty Effect of In-Kind Transfers: A 'Good Idea' Gone Too Far?" *Policy Studies Journal*, vol. 10 (March 1982), p. 510.

a. Includes adjustment for simulated value of taxes and income underreporting.

b. Estimate from Peter Gottschalk and Sheldon Danziger, "Macroeconomic Conditions, Income Transfers, and the Trend in Poverty" (University of Wisconsin–Madison, Institute for Research on Poverty, September 1983), p. 13.

method is used. If food, housing, and medicaid benefits are valued at their full market value, only 10 percent of the whole population in 1982 would have been counted as poor, rather than the 15 percent counted by only cash incomes.[6]

The pattern of changes over time, however, is not greatly affected by the inclusion of in-kind benefits, no matter how they are valued (see table 7-2). On any measure, the incidence of poverty declined substantially between the 1960s and the early 1970s as economic growth reinforced the effects of increased cash and noncash assistance to the poor. For the balance of the 1970s poverty changed little, as the negative effects of slow growth and relatively high unemployment were offset by continued increases in cash and noncash transfers. Between 1979 and 1982 poverty increased; indeed the increase appears larger if in-kind benefits are included than if they are not.[7]

The Changing Composition of the Poor

Over the last two decades, the characteristics of the poor population have changed. A smaller proportion of the poor is

6. If an adjustment is made for value to the recipient, the comparable figure is 12.7 percent. U.S. Bureau of the Census, *Technical Paper 51*, "Estimates of Poverty Including the Value of Noncash Benefits: 1979 to 1982" (GPO, 1984), p. 3.

7. Ibid.

aged now than in the 1960s. A larger proportion is in families headed by a woman without a husband, and a smaller percentage is in families headed by a working male. These changing demographic characteristics of the poor affect the choice of appropriate policies for reducing poverty.

The Elderly Poor

The most dramatic reductions in poverty have been among the elderly. In 1967 about 30 percent of those over age sixty-five had incomes below the poverty line—more than twice the rate for nonelderly persons. The incidence of poverty among the elderly dropped precipitously in the early 1970s when social security benefits were increased rapidly in real terms, and benefits have stayed roughly constant since then. Slightly more than 14 percent of those over sixty-five had cash incomes below the poverty line in 1982—a lower incidence of poverty than for the rest of the population.

Although the elderly make up a larger portion of the total population than they did in the 1960s, they represent a smaller fraction of the poor. The proportion of the poverty population that is elderly has fallen from 19 percent in 1967 to about 11 percent in 1982.

The aged receive relatively small amounts of earned income, and their participation in the labor force and reliance on earnings have declined substantially in recent years.[8] The reduction in poverty among the elderly is attributable to increases in the cash transfer programs specifically directed at this age group, especially social security and supplemental security income (SSI). In-kind benefits, especially medicare, have also been important. Because the elderly rely heavily on transfers, they are insulated from the impact of the business cycle. The elderly are the only demographic group that experienced no rise in poverty in either the 1975–76 or the 1979–82 recession.

---

8. Labor force participation rates for the elderly have been nearly halved since 1960. See Bureau of Labor Statistics, *Labor Force Statistics Derived from the Current Population Survey: A Databook*, vol. 1, BLS Bulletin 2096 (GPO, 1982), p. 611. The percentage of elderly household heads receiving earnings income has fallen correspondingly, from 52 percent to 44 percent over 1974–82.

Nonelderly Poor Families

A major change in the living arrangements of Americans has occurred in the last two decades and is having an exaggerated impact on the population in poverty. The traditional husband-and-wife family is less prevalent than it used to be, while families headed by a woman with no husband have become more common. The percentage of family members living in husband-and-wife families dropped from 91 percent in 1965 to 86 percent in 1982, while the proportion living in families headed by women rose from 9 to 14 percent.

This shift is even more apparent for children under the age of eighteen: the percentage living in families headed by females nearly doubled between 1965 and 1982, while the proportion living in two-parent families fell from 90 to 80 percent.

This shift may be viewed with alarm as reflecting a breakdown of traditional values or more positively as reflecting increased freedom and opportunity for women, but there is no question that it has changed the nature of the poverty problem. Women who head families are less likely to be in the labor force than men, and they have substantially lower earnings. They are much more likely to be poor. Increasingly, statistics reveal the "feminization" of poverty.

In the 1960s most poor families were headed by husbands or other males. Many of these men were employed at low-wage jobs and did not earn enough to keep their families out of poverty. Rising wage levels reduced the incidence of poverty among these families and, combined with the changing family structure for the whole population, substantially reduced the proportion of poor families with male heads.

The percentage of poor persons in families headed by a male was reduced by roughly one-third from 1960 to 1979, falling from 80 to 53 percent. The proportion of poor persons in families headed by a working male also fell dramatically over the same period, from 67 percent to 34 percent. Since 1979 poverty among families headed by males has increased again, but this increase may have been a recession phenomenon and will probably be reversed if growth continues.

The incidence of poverty among households headed by

females fell slowly over 1960–79 and rose again in 1979–82. The proportion of all families headed by women was rising in this period and the proportion of poor families with female heads rose even faster. Forty-three percent of all poor families were headed by nonelderly women in 1982.

For blacks, the figures are even more striking. More than two-thirds of poor black families are headed by women. Three-fourths of poor black children live in such families.

Like the aged, poor households headed by females depend heavily upon transfers for the income they receive. The transfer programs upon which these households rely—primarily AFDC and some forms of general assistance—have not maintained their real dollar value as well as those upon which the elderly rely. Thus, even though both the elderly and households headed by females depend heavily upon transfer income, poverty rates for the former group continued to fall through 1982, while the rate for the latter went up after 1979.

The feminization of poverty is a worrisome trend, since economic growth alone is unlikely to have a major impact on this group. One study of the means by which families escape poverty found that a female family head was only half as likely as a male family head to end a spell of poverty because of increases in the head's earnings. Conversely, female family heads left poverty more than three times as often as male family heads as a result of increases in unearned (transfer) income.[9]

Policies to Reduce Poverty

The lessons of the last few years make clear that recession can make poverty worse, especially if transfer programs are restrained at the same time. But the composition of the low-income population gives little reason to expect a substantial decline in poverty even if growth is sustained. The group that makes up the largest and fastest-growing share of the poverty

9. Mary Jo Bane and David T. Ellwood, "Slipping Into and Out of Poverty: The Dynamics of Spells," National Bureau of Economic Research Working Paper 1199 (Cambridge, Mass.: NBER, September 1983).

population—families headed by females—will probably experience little reduction in poverty from economic growth alone. One study finds that with exclusive reliance on growth rather than some combination of growth and transfers to reduce poverty, it may take as long as eleven years to get poverty rates back down to where they were in 1979.[10] That is too long.

In the short run the most direct approach to easing the plight of the poor is to increase benefits going explicitly to poor people, especially those programs that have failed to keep up with the cost of living. Benefits could be targeted to those most in need without major restructuring of current programs. Several transfer options are described below, together with a proposal for shifting more of the cost of support of low-income children onto the absent parent.

Although cash transfers may be the most direct way to reduce poverty, they are not necessarily the most desirable in the long run, from either the point of view of the poor or that of the taxpayer. It would be far better to help the poor acquire the skills and the opportunities they need to be self-supporting. However, training and job placement programs for the poor have had mixed success in the past and are unlikely to produce positive results if unemployment is high. In the growing economy that we hope will result from improved economic policy, however, new efforts should be made to increase the chances that more of the poor can become self-supporting.

Some of these proposals will require considerable expenditures by the federal government. The plan we have offered in earlier chapters for reducing the deficit includes sufficient funding to allow programs for the poor (AFDC, food stamps, and SSI) to be maintained at their real 1982 value. We believe that more needs to be done, as we suggest below, but in the interest of keeping deficits down, we believe that further expenditures should be financed by additional tax revenues or savings from other areas of the budget.

10. Gottschalk and Danziger, "Macroeconomic Conditions, Income Transfers, and the Trend in Poverty," p. 30. They used a model based on some rather optimistic assumptions (sustained 3 percent per year real growth in GNP and transfers maintained constant at 1982 levels).

Transfer Programs

The following four proposals would reduce poverty directly by increasing benefits for those who are especially needy or are excluded from present programs.[11]

1. Establish a national minimum benefit for AFDC. AFDC benefit levels vary greatly among states. Even when combined with food stamps, benefit levels in low-benefit states are far below the poverty line. Bringing the combined AFDC and food stamp benefits for a family with no earnings up to three-fourths of the poverty line would directly increase the incomes of about a million and half families with children at a combined state and federal cost of $2 billion to $3 billion.

2. Increase food stamp benefits. An uncomplicated way to increase the income of a broad range of low-income people quickly would be to raise the maximum benefit for food stamps, now set well below the poverty level. Food stamps are available to almost all poor households, including many who are ineligible for public assistance because they contain two parents or do not include children. Raising the food stamp maximum payment by $4 per month per beneficiary would cost about $1 billion.

3. Cover low-income families with children under medicaid. Many poor families with children are not eligible for medicaid because they do not qualify for public assistance. These include working poor families with two parents and AFDC families who have worked their way off welfare but still have incomes too low to provide adequate health care for their children. Extending medicaid coverage to all families with children and incomes below the poverty line would cost the federal government about $6 billion a year and the states another $5 billion under present cost-sharing arrangements, but even a more limited program would be of substantial help to needy families and might improve the health of children in low-income families.

4. Increase the earned-income tax credit. Although the federal

11. Testimony of Rudolph G. Penner before the Subcommittees on Oversight and on Public Assistance and Unemployment Compensation of the House Committee on Ways and Means, October 18, 1983.

income tax largely exempts those with income below the poverty line, increased reliance on payroll, sales, and property taxes at the federal, state, and local levels has increased tax burdens on the poor in recent years. The fact that the earned-income tax credit is not indexed has eroded that form of assistance for the working poor. When tax rates were cut across the board in 1981, no mention was made of the earned-income tax credit. In addition, while automatic indexation of income tax brackets is set to begin in 1985 to adjust for future inflation, no such provisions have been made for the earned-income tax credit.[12] An immediate upward revision of the credit to adjust for past inflation and permanent indexing would seem the logical remedy.

Part of the cost of increasing assistance to low-income families with children could be offset if a more vigorous national effort were made to require absent parents to contribute to the support of their children. One such proposal has been called the social child support program (SCSP).[13] The SCSP would reduce some of the complications and cost of the present welfare system by shifting some of the burden for the child's support onto the absent parent. A simple payroll deduction (scaled to income) from the absent parent's wages would be supplemented with a federal subsidy should the revenue fall below a certain minimum. The SCSP effectively nationalizes what a number of states already do: require absent parents to pay for child support. A federal program along these lines would have two distinct advantages over a myriad of state plans: first, an absent parent could not evade financial responsibility by moving to another state; and second, the Internal Revenue Service and social security mechanisms could be employed to locate noncustodial parents and enforce payment in a way states are unable to do presently. The potential savings in AFDC payments resulting from national implementation of the SCSP could be as high as $1.5 billion.

12. See *General Explanation of the Economic Recovery Act of 1981 (H.R. 4242, 97th Congress; Public Law 97-34)*, prepared by the Joint Committee on Taxation, 97 Cong. 1 sess. (GPO, 1981), pp. 20–32, 38–40.

13. For a more detailed explanation of the program, see Irwin Garfinkel, "The Role of Child Support in Antipoverty Policy," IRP Discussion Paper 713-82 (University of Wisconsin–Madison, Institute for Research on Poverty, October 1982).

Training and Work

In an improving economy with declining unemployment rates, well-designed job training and placement programs stand a better chance of success than they would have in a low-growth economy with high unemployment. We believe a major new effort should be made to try new approaches to helping low-income people move out of poverty through employment. Efforts should be concentrated on teenagers and low-income mothers.

If the economy continues to grow and unemployment declines, the next few years will offer an unusual opportunity to break the cycle of poverty by concentrating on improving the education, training, job experience, and motivation of young people from low-income families. The opportunity arises from the fact that there will be fewer young people entering the labor force than there have been in recent years. Hence it should be easier for new entrants, including those from low-income families, to find jobs.

Young people, typically from families headed by females, now represent a significant part of the poverty population. Some of them make it into the mainstream of American society, but many have dim futures: they drop out of school with few skills and little ability to compete for jobs; a substantial fraction are functionally illiterate; and many are teenage girls who have become mothers themselves. Unemployment rates for these low-income teenagers are appallingly high. Young people without job skills (and with children themselves) quickly become the next welfare generation.

Yet relatively little emphasis has been put on helping this age group. Compensatory education has focused primarily on preschool and elementary school children. Summer job programs for youths have had some success, as have some in-school programs. But in recent years high unemployment rates and competition from large numbers of better-skilled, better-educated young people have stacked the deck against disadvantaged teenagers. The next few years could be different, however. Unlike the 1970s, when especially large numbers of young people entered the labor force, the late 1980s and early

1990s will see unusually small numbers of new entrants. If general unemployment declines, intensive efforts to improve high school education in poor areas and to help students gain work experience while staying in school may pay off in substantial reductions in the number of new families entering the poverty cycle.[14]

Studies have shown that youths who have both early employment experience and a satisfactory high school education will fare better in future employment than youths possessing only one of these job market credentials. A subminimum wage for high school students might increase job opportunities for young people, but might also provide an incentive for students to quit school and thereby lose one of these credentials. One study, the Youth Incentive Entitlement Pilot Projects (YIEPP), combined both school and work experience in an attempt to ensure that youths would obtain both credentials.[15]

The program was targeted to teenagers from low-income families, both those still in high school and those who had left school before graduation. A guaranteed job at the federal minimum wage (part time during the school year, full time during the summer) was provided so long as the youth remained in (or returned to) school and achieved satisfactory performance in both school and work. More than half of the eligible youths in each pilot area participated in the program, and despite some problems of coordination among schools, employers, and program sponsors, the results were very promising. Implementation of the program nationally could cost between $624 million and $1.8 billion. This is an expensive proposal but one with substantial potential for long-term benefits.

In addition, renewed efforts should be made to help low-

14. Growth in the share of the population aged sixteen to twenty-four will be negative through 1995. For example, over 1985–90, the number of males aged sixteen to twenty-four will fall 2.13 percent, while the number of females will fall 2.07 percent. See Howard N. Fullerton, "The 1995 Labor Force: A First Look," *Monthly Labor Review*, vol. 103 (December 1980), p. 14. Because birthrates have begun to rise again in recent years, such an ideal opportunity may not last long and may not present itself again for some time to come.

15. See William A. Diaz, Joseph Ball, and Carl Wolfhagen, *Linking School and Work for Disadvantaged Youths, the YIEPP Demonstration: Final Implementation Report* (New York: Manpower Demonstration Research Corporation, 1982) for details of the project.

income parents earn enough to move their families out of poverty. To increase the attractiveness of work to parents in families eligible for AFDC, some changes in tax policy and some new emphasis on federal job training programs will be necessary. The present income tax code provides a credit for child day-care expenses. To take advantage of this, however, a single parent must earn enough to make it worthwhile to file a tax return. In the interest of simplifying the tax system in the manner outlined in chapter 5, such a deduction should be eliminated and replaced with a universal, taxable grant to cover both formal and informal child-care and work-related expenses.

These changes will do little to reduce poverty, however, unless they are accompanied by both employment counseling and job placement efforts. The National Supported Work Demonstration was quite successful in preparing AFDC-eligible female parents for work experience, and did so at a cost roughly equivalent to that of providing public service employment under the Comprehensive Employment and Training Act.[16]

Such a supported work program would be considerably more expensive than simply providing a grant to cover child day-care expenses. The potential benefits to the individual are great, however, in terms of increased employment, hours worked, and earnings. An additional benefit accrues to society from such a program: a reduction in both welfare dependency and welfare payments. The cost of national implementation of this program could produce significant savings in AFDC, food stamp, and rental housing subsidies and thereby defray much of the program cost. These benefits and the great handicaps with which this group would otherwise enter the labor market may well justify the expense.

Conclusion

In earlier chapters, we have advocated policies to ensure sustained economic growth and an easier adjustment to growth in the coming years. Though the plight of the poor has mirrored

16. See Manpower Demonstration Research Corporation, *Summary and Findings of the National Supported Work Demonstration* (Cambridge, Mass.: Ballinger, 1980), p. 151. In fact, of four "hard-to-employ" groups, the AFDC parents fared best.

the plight of the general economy in recent years—progress in the 1960s, stagnation in the 1970s, and retrogression in the 1979–82 recession—there is no guarantee that this parallelism will prevail as the economy grows in the future.

Progress made against poverty before 1979 resulted from the combination of expanding employment opportunities and strong growth in transfer programs. Now, however, poverty is more concentrated in groups that may be unable to take advantage of the expanded opportunities that should result from simple economic growth—particularly minorities, female family heads, and unskilled youths. At the same time, transfer programs that had previously helped those with little attachment to the market economy have experienced sharp real cutbacks.

The prospects for reducing poverty solely through growth in the next few years are thus bleak. But this diagnosis suggests a prescription: creating new initiatives in job training, eliminating the barriers to work faced by the poor, and resuming real growth in transfer programs to help those still unable to earn enough to keep out of poverty. The cost of such an agenda is not insignificant, but it is a price worth paying to ensure that the economic growth we have advocated is more widely shared.